AUTHOR BIOGRAPHY

John Bayley is the author of *Alice*, *The Queer Captain*, *George's Lair* and *The Red Hat*. *Iris: A Memoir*, described by the *Observer* as 'the greatest love story of our age', was published in paperback by Abacus in 1999. John Bayley was Warton Professor of English at the University of Oxford and is a fellow of St Catherine's College.

Also by John Bayley in Abacus:

IRIS: A MEMOIR OF IRIS MURDOCH

IRIS
AND THE FRIENDS

A Year of Memories

John Bayley

An *Abacus* Book

First published in Great Britain by
Gerald Duckworth & Co. Ltd in 1999
This edition published by Abacus in 2000

A CIP catalogue record for this book
is available from the British Library.

ISBN 0 349 11310 6

Acknowledgements

Lines by Edith Sitwell from *The Collected Poems*
published by Sinclair Stevenson reproduced by permission
of David Higham Associates.

Extracts from the work of John Betjeman from
'Spring in North Oxford' and 'Youth and Age on Beaulieu River, Hants'
reproduced by permission of John Murray (Publishers) Ltd.

Typeset by Palimpsest Book Production Limited,
Polmont, Stirlingshire
Printed and bound in Great Britain by
Clays Ltd, St Ives plc

Abacus
A Division of
Little, Brown and Company (UK)
Brettenham House
Lancaster Place
London WC2E 7EN

Contents

PART I

MEMORY

1

I can hardly believe it's all over. At the end it happened so quickly. My diary says that Iris and I were still together, struggling along together, in the peculiar way that an Alzheimer patient and carer do, less than three weeks ago.

And then between one day and the next it became all but impossible to get her to eat and drink. I coaxed her in every way I could think of, but she seemed abruptly to have given up being a good if sometimes difficult child, and became a sadly but politely determined adult. Politely and smilingly she declined to open her mouth to have a teaspoon or the edge of a cup put in. As if she had decided it was no longer worthwhile.

With the brain gone can the body take over the power of decision? It looked like it. What Pascal said of the heart may be true of the body too? Like the heart it has its own reasons, which reason knows nothing about? If no one interferes, it knows how to do the right thing at the right moment?

And that is surely very comforting? For whom do I mean? For the onlooker of course, the carer. The patient is already far off. In a dark country where they have their own ways of knowing things. And doing things.

*   *   *

JOHN BAYLEY

One night some months ago, in the autumn of '98 it must have been, I had woken up suddenly with the feeling that something was wrong. I switched on my pencil torch and found it was two o'clock. I'd been asleep two hours. I felt bemused, but at the same time intensely wakeful. For there was a subdued noise somewhere in the house. The sound of voices.

Was it burglars? But why should burglars be talking? Did they think the house was empty? I reached over to the other side of the bed. There was nothing there. Iris had gone.

She's always such a good sleeper! That was my first thought. In its earlier stages Alzheimer's Disease actually seems to confer minor physical compensations. The sufferers may sleep soundly, look well, never get a cold. Iris liked to go to bed early and slept almost without stirring until eight or nine in the morning. So what had gone wrong?

And whom was she talking to? Surprising how eerie her voice sounded, in the silence of the night, coming up muffled from somewhere downstairs. No words to recognise. There wouldn't, in any case, be intelligible words: and no doubt that's why it sounded like two or three people, conversing together, voices merging.

Who were these new friends of Iris, with whom she was chatting as if they were already old friends?

My heart sank inside me as I realised that the disease must have entered another phase. Sometimes in the early morning Iris has got up to go to the loo. As I might do: as anyone might do. But wandering round the house and chatting to herself at two in the morning was a new development.

For a moment I thought I heard the voice of Macbeth, the most terrifyingly intimate of all Shakespeare's tragic characters. 'Methought I heard a voice cry "Sleep no more!"' One is apt to get such dramatic visions of despair into one's head at two in the morning.

It passed. Daylight came. A bit of sleep for both of us. And a little later that morning I had a visitation. Perhaps it was one of Iris's nocturnal friends? Or perhaps it was Dr Alzheimer's very particular, very special intimate, who in time would become the friend of us both . . .

Doctor Alois Alzheimer, a native of Alsace, wrote a treatise in 1907 on the disease or condition that is named after him. He had observed it in patients who were in their fifties as well as in older people, and he had concluded that this type of dementia differed from more generalised aspects of senility. The condition was also marked by a regular progression, which might be either rapid or slow; but he found no cases of remission or recovery.

A bleak outlook, which left not much room for lightness of heart in the sufferer, or for those who attended the sufferer? Not necessarily. There may be rewards and alleviations on the way, for all parties. As well as anxiety in the patient there may be a kind of merciful indifference, even lightness of heart, a shrugging off of responsibility for the things most of us feel we have to do every day – washing, dressing, keeping up appearances.

Even the good doctor's name, ill-omened as it might

seem, can possess a droll freedom of association. Remove it into other circumstances and it could signify other and more cheerful things, more comical things even. 'The Alzheimer', a potent vintage racing car which in its time even challenged the Bugatti? A gambling club, a select restaurant? Or a youthful hostess might candidly admit, when a guest praised the pâté, that she had got it at Alzheimer's . . .

Bad situations survive on jokes. That was the point of trench humour. If they are in close contact with one another carer and patient can even share such things. I will tell my thoughts, such as they are, to Iris; and she will smile at me when she sees from my face that I am wandering off into some sort of fantasy.

It is possible for both of us to have friends in common with Dr Alzheimer, who certainly does have his friends. And now it's as if my own memories were becoming Iris's friends too.

On that morning last winter I was fully conscious that Iris's affliction had suddenly entered a new and ominous phase. I did not know it would be all but the final one. At the time I was more aware of what I now think of as a visitation.

Perhaps it started in my head as a kind of joke? Perhaps I came to associate the joke later not with Dr Alzheimer himself but with a delightful and humorous man, a real doctor from the Warneford Hospital, who although he was immensely busy came regularly to call during the final stages of Iris's illness. A true scholar and healer, as well as the kindest of men. It was he who saw when the time had come, the moment when we had to get Iris into a home as soon as possible.

But on that morning, after her night out downstairs, Iris was peacefully asleep. I went down to the kitchen and made myself a mug of green tea. 'Gunpowder' tea. Each curly dark-green leaf expands to unexpected size in the boiling water, like a Japanese paper flower. In its dry unexpanded state it must have looked to those early tea merchants like a grain of gunpowder.

I've become partial to it in the early morning. Should be made weak, when it's mild and delicious. Said to be good for the heart. Good for the memory perhaps too.

Coming up from the kitchen with my mug of tea I caught the tail of my vest on the arm of a kitchen chair. Over the years the vest has become ragged, with a sizeable hole at the back. I pulled at it like a dog pulling at the lead, but this did not help. I put the tea down, wriggled around, and managed at last to unhook the vest from the arm of the windsor chair – a chair polished by more than forty years of me sitting in it.

We bought the chair cheap at a junkshop in 1957, the year after we were married. The proprietor had showed us its wormholes with a great appearance of candour, and went on to sell us a little can of some chemical treatment, with a tube and nozzle which had to be inserted into each wormhole in turn.

Iris did this conscientiously for more than a week, like the priestess of some strange cult. And the chair still hangs together, so perhaps her labours were not in vain.

*   *   *

[7]

Such a visit was indeed more like a visitation. Even an annunciation. When I got back upstairs with my tea Iris was still peacefully asleep. I looked at her quiet face, remembering that ancient time, and the zeal with which she had manipulated her little can of chemical. And there was something else too, trying to get into my mind. What was it?

Proust was quite right about the onset of memory, although his theory of it soon begins to sound rather too portentous. But it is sudden, and it is unexpected. It is also a source of joy.

Back in bed beside Iris I lay and thought of that moment when I had freed the tail of my vest from the arm of the windsor chair. The moment was bringing something back to me. But what was it? I looked for inspiration at the dear creature asleep beside me, but it was nothing to do with her . . .

And then I remembered. Sleeping and at peace at last as she was, she had brought me this visitation. Even though it came from a much earlier time, a time long before she knew me.

Lying back, relaxed now and sipping, I found I was on the golf course of my childhood. The golf course of Littlestone-on-Sea. But I was not trying to play golf. It was the family game, but I had always managed to avoid it. I had other things to do on the golf course.

At that moment I was slinking furtively through the thick seaside grass – 'the rough' – at the side of the course. I was making for an old and derelict brick cottage, which lay in the no-man's-land between the golf course and the fields and dykes of Romney Marsh.

Perhaps it had once been a smugglers' lair? Perhaps it still was? I had been reading about their exploits. The book was *Dr Syn*, by Russell Thorndike, brother, as I later discovered, of the famous actress, Sybil Thorndike. *Dr Syn* must have appeared in 1931, when I was six. Perhaps 1932.

But I was not much interested in smugglers as such. It was the place itself, its nearness and its otherness. It was close to the links, where dedicated golfers in plus-fours selected and swung their clubs, but it seemed all the more remote and strange for that, in a world of its own.

And what preoccupied me at that moment was something quite different from smugglers or golfers. It was mantraps. I knew that these diabolical contrivances had once been set among long grass to catch poachers, and why not to catch smugglers too? I knew it, because one rainy morning I had opened a book on the shelves of our seaside house. I hardly registered the title at the time, but it must have been Hardy's novel, *The Woodlanders*.

It opened at the page on which the heroine, skimming lightly along a woodland path, just escapes the jaws of a mantrap. Her foot touches the plate and sets off the trap, but so swift and lissom is she that her ankles evade the clash of the serrated iron jaws as they spring together. Not so her trailing skirts however. Pulled down by them, she finds herself helpless in the monster's grasp. Unable to move, she is compelled at length to abandon decorum and contrive to slip out of her silk dress and her petticoats. The scene then shifted to her estranged husband, awaiting her in the midnight gloom at their agreed rendezvous.

But distraught wives and estranged husbands were not an exciting topic. Having established the heroine's safety I lost interest and put the book back in its place. *Dr Syn*, which I had already twice devoured, fascinated me much more. Not only was one of the miniature engines on the Romney Hythe and Dymchurch Light Railway called after him, but in the book he was a local parson, admired by his flock, who had been a pirate and was now secretly a smuggler. I could appreciate that. I loved the deceit of it, and the enigmatic figure of Dr Syn himself. Perhaps the ruined cottage would turn out to be his private lair?

It was twenty years or so before I actually read *The Woodlanders*. Had I been six or seven years older when I found it in our seaside cottage I might have been more intrigued by the heroine's predicament, as she sped on agitatedly to her rendezvous, clad only in her vest and drawers. It must have given her husband a thrill, and no doubt assisted in their subsequent reconciliation. Hardy was very well aware of the graphic and dramatic possibilities of female underwear in his plots. For a Victorian he sailed quite close to the wind on this occasion, and on another too: in his early novel *A Pair of Blue Eyes*, he has the heroine remove all her underclothing to make a rope to rescue her fiancé, who is clinging precariously to the edge of a cliff.

But at the age of eight, even though I was nearly nine, female underwear had no special charms. Mantraps were the thing. They equally thrilled and alarmed my imagination. And so I approached the ruined cottage with exaggerated care. Who knew what might lie concealed in the thick marsh grass around it? Partly in the story I was telling myself inside my head, partly in sober reality, I was relieved to reach the crumbling brick wall of the cottage unscathed, untrapped. I could now see a sort of hatch in the wall like a miniature barn door, not very high up. I gave the side of it a tentative pull, and with a creak it swung open. I was mentally prepared for smugglers, but not for the apparition now confronting me. Two foot in front of my face sat a large living creature. It had a snowy white breast and huge dark eyes. We stared at each other. Then it swept over my head and flew across the marsh, a soundless brown shadow.

It had all come from the moment when I had freed the tail of my vest from the arm of the windsor chair. I had wriggled out of the trap, like Hardy's heroine.

Iris was still peacefully asleep, lying on her back, giving an occasional little snore or grunt. Beside her I sipped my tea, and abandoned myself to thoughts of that summertime at Littlestone, the ruined cottage, Dr Syn, the great barn owl . . .

Consciously and greedily I gave myself up to these memories. The habit of memory has become a real solace now. Almost, one might say, a fix. Especially in the early morning. With Iris still sweetly and childishly asleep, still unafflicted with the compulsions of Alzheimer's, which will cause her on bad mornings, and most mornings are bad, to shed silent miserable tears, or to utter small anxious cries and queries on waking.

'Where is? We going? Then go? Where this?' I shall stroke her, soothe her down. With luck she may go to sleep

again. If she does I shall plunge back into the flow of memory, as if I were slipping down the bank and into a cool river, on a hot day.

Later on I shall be able to attend to Iris with one part of my mind while continuing to meander about in my own thoughts. But they will not then be so vivid or so complete, so almost sensually satisfying as they can be at this early hour. It reminds me of one of the devils in *Paradise Lost*, who while his more heroic companions are planning a hazardous vengeance upon God, only wants to be left safe to think his own thoughts. Milton speaks on his behalf with great eloquence.

> For who would lose
> Though full of pain, this intellectual being,
> These thoughts that wander through eternity? . . .

Never mind eternity: I am quite content to wander back to actual years and months, actual places. But when Iris wakes up they will have to vanish, at least for the moment. I cannot make the right noises, and deliver reassurance, while they are going on. Something in what's left of Iris's mind would know that her anxieties were not being paid full attention to; and they would increase.

Alzheimer's is implacable: it grows worse all the time, but insensibly. It is only by thinking back a few months, or looking in my diary, that I can register the changes. But as the condition grows worse, and its successive stages more difficult to cope with, compensations multiply.

[12]

It is these I think of as the friends. Iris's and mine. Dr A's too. Some are mutual. Today we can still cuddle together; we still enjoy lucid jokey moments, small bouts of pleasure in each other, at each other. But many more now have to be solitary, unshareable. It is no use trying to tell Iris about these memories as I would once have done, no use trying out an idea or a thought on her. It upsets her; a bothered look can come over her face, but usually there is only vacancy and, with luck, a smile.

Last year, 1997, I wrote a book about Iris, our past life and our present one. Worse as the condition now is, we can still go along living alone together. The certainty of things getting worse is our most unexpected friend; yet undoubtedly he is one. And I suppose it is the friend who sharpens an appetite for living in the past, gives the process a kind of connoisseurship. Someone with cancer once told me of the relief he felt when he refused further therapy, although doctors urged him to stick with it. The future had ceased to concern him. He was free to think only of the past.

Iris is awake. Her endless fidgets and queries begin to empty my mind. I must summon up logic and language, and reply properly. At this time of day she relies – paradoxically – on what seem to be real answers: jokes and nonsense – old chums as they are – won't do.

I sometimes say, 'Don't worry, darling, we shall soon be dead.' This makes a silence, but not exactly a restful one. Is Iris thinking about it? Does the word still mean something? I have no way to find out.

I do not regard suicide or euthanasia as Iris's friends,

or as friends of Dr A. Belial, that unheroic devil in *Paradise Lost*, would not have approved of them either. He deprecated his fellow devils' heroic wish to immolate themselves in the destruction of heaven and earth. He was for life, at any price; he knew that as things get worse the life of the mind can seem ever more and more worth having.

And yet I have had frequent thoughts of doing ourselves in together, if there were a nice safe reliable way.

The writer Arthur Koestler and his wife did that. He was ailing and had cancer: she was young and in good health, but she wanted to go with him. Hard to understand, and yet there it was. Would she have had second thoughts the next day, if there had been a next day? Like impulse buys in the supermarket, most suicides only seemed a good idea at the time, for the time?

In a sense it has all happened before. Iris's mother succumbed in her eighties to what was then called senile dementia. No reason to suppose it hereditary; no fear then it might affect her daughter too. But as Iris's mother began to go round the bend, her minder Jack amassed on her behalf a collection of sleeping pills. Barbiturates: the real thing. A host of blood-red capsules. After her death I found and appropriated them, thinking they might come in handy one day. If they still worked. They must be somewhere in the house, but in this house, or any house we've ever lived in, I would be most unlikely to find them.

We used to have a phrase for it: 'Gone to Pieland.' Once we had bought a pork pie, a very fine pie indeed, from some superior delicatessen. We put it on the table to eat for supper, and when the moment came the pie had gone. It has not been seen since.

Resolving itself back into its contingent ingredients the pie seemed to have gone to a happier place. Perhaps to the 'Valley of Lost Things', once visited by the hero of Ariosto's mock-heroic epic, *Orlando Furioso*. Thank goodness that does not apply to those memories of the distant past which now keep me going.

Iris is awake, and mental life must be suspended. I give a last wistful glimpse back at the barn owl, the ruined cottage on the links, the mantrap fantasy . . . What took place in my head when I hooked my tail on the chair seemed involuntary, a sensation too immediate for pleasure. Only afterwards, when I got back to bed, did I begin to enjoy it.

Proust must have been the same. He dramatises the joy he received from that sudden flooding back of the past, its recapture through the cake in the tea (how disgusting that combination sounds!) and the way he knocked his foot against an irregular piece of pavement. But I feel sure that he had to arrange such things quietly in his mind before he began really to enjoy them. Proust never saw a television set but the process seems to me now a little like sitting down in front of one's own private television screen, and turning it on. Total recall at my age seems a very deliberate process.

And Belial, that insinuating devil, was surely right?

But never mind the present; it is saying goodbye to one's life in the past that would make one think twice about suicide, however simple and easy its process. Leaving the present would be nothing: it has no shadow and no substance, no memory power either. When addressing an envelope the other day I came to a sudden stop. The letter was to somebody I knew well, and I'd written his first name.

What's the other? It's gone. It will be back in a few minutes but in the meantime I want to post the damned letter and be rid of it. The life of the present is full of such exasperations, riddled too with angst, alienation, fear of contemporary life. Fifty, even forty years ago, everything was so much better?

Well, naturally. If we had grandchildren the present time might not seem so repulsive, so vulgar, so swiftly decaying, so full of daily dread and dislike. I can't imagine having had a family, but I suppose what they say must be true. We are born to reproduce, and to find satisfaction when old in the thought of those others' future. Though I avoid children, even I can see that they cannot help finding this world a wonderful place, and some of that continuing wonder must, as it were, rub off on their grandparents?

How would Iris feel about it, if she did feel nowadays? Even in the midst of the poor darling's endless agitations – banging on the front windows to alert passersby, jerking endlessly at the locked front door, carrying clothes and cutlery round the house – there does seem to remain a core of serenity, in her smile, in the response to a tease, which I can't find anywhere in myself.

Illusion? Or is that still centre, from around which everything else has departed, another of the friends, come to drop in on us at this stage of Iris's dark journey? Nearly five years now since the first symptoms declared themselves.

They are trying to find out, so a doctor told me, what it is that Alzheimer patients actually die of. Physically they can appear in good health; but they do die, usually within seven or eight years of diagnosis, and seemingly of nothing in particular, although pneumonia steps in at the end. The last of the friends.

So what about hastening the process? Couldn't we do it together, as I said? I may forget names when addressing envelopes, but there are two names as firmly in my head as any steadfast memory of childhood. Dr Alzheimer of course: he is in my mind every day, as the badge of the society called after him is in my buttonhole. But there is another name too.

Dr Kevorkian. A strange, saturnine name. Dr Kevorkian, death's angel, often pops up in newspaper features, showing off his polythene apparatus, teaching his fragile willing victims to do it themselves. Surely too he must be a boon and companion of our old pal Dr A? That might seem suitable?

But no: on reflection he certainly isn't a friend – very much the opposite. Dr A's rewards and compensations, even the most unexpected ones, are concerned with being alive; finding out not only how much there is in being alive, but what surprising *new* things there turn out to be: freedoms, and pleasures in constraint, which we would never have imagined or thought of, never even have considered possible.

'Sweet are the uses of adversity.' The commonest,

sanest Shakespearean wisdom. And yet it doesn't seem like adversity exactly. Just the way things are, or have become. That ever present need to escape, Dr A's most elusive friend, can only be implemented in the mind.

If I had a stroke or broke an arm I should be frantic to get back to Iris. If Iris were 'taken away' I would hardly know what to do. This is obvious, but it is less easy to grasp the inner point: that I have been embarked on a way of life, and could hardly find another one now. What would become of the mind, the memories I cling to now, if I were free to do as I wanted? Free to go anywhere and do anything?

I cannot imagine Iris without me. Just as I cannot imagine myself without her. She is always there, and so am I: she cannot do without me. Now I tell her I am going to the loo or into the kitchen, and she gazes at me anxiously, and tries to come. When I evade her she stands very close, fretting and peering. The objects she is usually carrying have the look of empty space, no longer having a purpose. Even if they are ordinary cups or knives and forks.

As her condition worsened, and our imprisonment became more complete, the compensations mounted up – they had to. For her as well as for me? I can hope so, at least. We both still have our small pleasures, which have become happily and mutually important: more and more important, not only because they are all we have left but because we can still share them.

When Beau Brummell, once the law-giver of high society's dress and behaviour, lost all his money and began to go mad, he took pleasure in walking on the beach at Boulogne, where he had fled to escape his creditors. He picked up seashells, carried them home to his lodgings, and experimented in restoring their brightness by painting them with vinegar.

As I watch Iris absorbed in the twigs and bits of paper she has picked up on our walks, I enter more and more into what she seems to be feeling. I look serious with her as she does it. We bend our heads together over what she has found.

2

Littlestone-on-Sea. The flat bright wastes of shore; the huge pale sky above the marsh. Our holiday home was behind the sea-wall, a curved concrete embankment above the sand and shingle. When the tide was up the sea was above our heads as we stood in the garden. Tamarisk and Euonymus bushes grew there, but not much else. Holes and small flags had been inserted in the sparse lawn to make a miniature putting green, which we despised. There was a proper one outside the club buildings by the golf course.

My brothers were both keen golfers. (In those days some of the more elderly members of the club used to pronounce the word as 'goffers'.) During our summer holidays two eighteen-hole rounds, morning and after-noon, were nothing to Michael and David; and they talked golfing technicalities at mealtimes with my father, a less dedicated performer who was none the less glad to see his sons devoting their energies so singlemindedly to the game.

But family toleration extended itself to me in the role of non-performer. It was somehow tacitly accepted that I need not seriously take part, all the more so as I was perfectly serious in paying lip homage to the game and listening with pleasure to their discussions. I also enjoyed 'walking round', as it was called; holding their clubs while they played a shot, and meanwhile daydreaming about my own concerns, such as the ruined cottage which I saw every morning as we processed along the fairway.

I was born in India in 1925, probably something of an afterthought. (My father was working for an oil company which never found any oil.) I felt different from the rest of the family, and they regarded me, but quite philosophically, as different too. At any date my brothers always seemed to me grown-up, whereas I was permanently childish.

My second brother Michael, nearly three years older, was easy both to admire and to get on with. I was very fond of him without knowing it, nor did he give signs of fondness for me. In our family, in any case, any demonstrations of affection were not so much disapproved of as assumed to be unnecessary and out of place. Michael tolerated my private world, and condescended at times to share in some of my secret fantasies and stratagems, although I would never have confided to him my most private ones, such as Dr Syn or the mantraps, or my ideas about the ruined cottage.

I never told him of my undercover visit there, nor of my unexpected confrontation with the great snowy-breasted owl. But in a good mood he was prepared to lay aside his bag of clubs on a fine evening, and indulge me in a stalking game. For this I took my sixpenny repeating cap pistols, a passable imitation of the Browning automatic.

I know that now, after seeing the real thing in the army, and I can feel retrospective surprise at how comparatively well-made these little toy guns were, even to the 'blueing' on the metal; and how cheap too, even by the deflationary standards of the thirties.

Michael, I accepted, was of an age to regard cap pistols as for the children. He had bought them for me at the village shop, where they also sold pingpong balls and fishing nets and buckets and spades, with his own pocket money. Naturally and properly he had more of it than I did, but it was a kind thing to do none the less. We kept the existence of these toy guns a secret from my parents, who would have strongly disapproved, my father particularly. He had been through the 1914–18 war, ending up as a major and battery commander in the field artillery. Like many ex-soldiers at the time he deplored warlike attitudes or national aggressiveness, although he was not in the least a pacifist. He would also have frowned upon his sons' showing what would have seemed to him a frivolous interest in the weapons of modern warfare.

Of course when the next war arrived he made passionate efforts to get back into the army and was highly upset that age and rheumatics stopped him. I think he secretly grudged his three sons' being in the army and he a civilian, although he was as devoutly grateful as my mother that all three survived; the eldest, David, becoming a prisoner of war in 1944, while Michael was wounded a few months later.

But such things were still what now seems to me a long way off, and in another world. What matters in my memories is that Michael bought me the cap pistols, and I was thrilled. I kept them well hidden and caressed them in secret. So much of childhood seems to have been spent in secret, and most of its pleasures came from this. Most of the memories I have of it too.

I already considered life to be far from wonderful; something, indeed, to be avoided as much as one could, like school or games or children's parties. Life, real life, was like a picture that frightened me seriously. It was represented for me on the cover of a magazine that I had read avidly, many times over. The magazine was called *Wings*, and consisted mostly of tales of aerial combat and reminiscences by pilots who had flown and fought in the Great War.

My eldest brother had managed to buy it surreptitiously on Ashford station, and it had come down to me after the pair of them had finished with it. They were rather superior about it but I was not. I was both frightened and fascinated. And my parents would have disapproved. I had been warned by both brothers to keep its existence a secret.

The coloured cover illustration showed not a 'Hun' Fokker or Albatros but an English SE 5, very meticulously drawn, going earthward in a slow slant, the pilot slumped forward over the controls. His leather helmet and sightless goggles haunted me, as did the streak of blood on the outside of the cockpit, where the dead arm rested. I associated that cover picture with the wax model of a dog, strapped down and stuck full of needles, which lolled realistically in the window of the Anti-Vivisection Society's premises, just off Trafalgar

Square. Both, I knew, represented what life, real life, was about.

In fact these two things did not so much frighten me as produce a dire and settled kind of hopelessness in the pit of my stomach. How different they were from the evening game with Michael, when we pretended to stalk and shoot each other on the deserted links. The Germans never won at those times and there were no shadows in the long evening sunlight. The turf of the fairway smelt of thyme, and in the immense arc of the sky, just beginning to glow a deeper blue, a lark or two was still singing. Here was romance and excitement, with no damage done. I knew it was all make-believe, and so much preferred it to the real thing.

I always lost the game, and really preferred losing it, without admitting this to myself, or of course to Michael. My usual idea was to lie on the brow of a big bunker, one of the few eminences on the links. I would be hidden in the tussocks of marram grass, able to see out, and all around. Or so I thought. In choosing this place I showed a touching ignorance of one of the cardinal points of military strategy: never do what the enemy expects you to do.

Lying there in the sunny evening I happily awaited the moment at which my unsuspecting brother should by rights appear, somewhere in front of me. In fact he usually managed to stalk me from behind, crawling silently until he was in range, and then startling me with a volley of gunfire, so that I surrendered on the spot. The shock and the surrender were equally delicious. At such moments he had a kind yet weary air, never seeming pleased with his victory or contemptuous of my own shortcomings as a tactician.

Once when he was slow in finding me, and I lay still a long time, a lark, still singing, dropped to its nest a few feet away. Their nests are so simply but effectively camouflaged – the brown speckled eggs nestled into a twist of matching grass – that they are impossible to find except by accident. From my lair I marked the spot, and when I had been duly flushed out and our stalking game was over, I found the nest and proudly showed it to Michael, who permitted himself to be interested in his kindly negligent way. We took none of the eggs – it would have seemed unsporting to both of us – but I was not above removing the occasional egg from a thrush's or linnet's nest that I found elsewhere. I never 'blew' the eggs, although in theory I knew how to. Their delicate round weight was part of their appeal to me, but my private egg collection, also concealed from my parents, was not an extensive or a methodical one.

Our house being a few feet from the sea we used to bathe in summer, always at high tide. My brothers could be lofty about this to them childish practice, alleging that it 'put the eye out', for golf. Both were in fact good swimmers, and sometimes Michael let me ride on his back to a raft which was moored for the summer some distance offshore. My father, who never bathed himself, was impatient at the way I kept in my depth with a toe safely on or near the sea bed, and offered me a pound note if I would swim back from the raft after Michael had carried me there. Although ashamed that I could not swim properly I never dared attempt to win the pound, although with my brothers giving me close escort back to the shore I knew I could easily have done so.

My father struck me as a melancholy man, although with the uninterested detachment of the age I then was I could not see why he should be. He had my mother after all, who loved him – I could see that, though again it did not interest me – and he had three fine sons. That was how it struck me one day, as we paraded, washed and combed, before some social event or other. I noticed how my father, in his dark blue summer jacket with brass buttons, eyed us in what seemed to me a surprisingly unenthusiastic way. Why should he think so little of his offspring? It did not occur to me that the reason might be that we were all boys, and he would have liked a girl, particularly as the youngest. Or perhaps there was some other reason. But that seems to me now the most probable one. Perhaps he did not know it himself. Perhaps he did not know he was a melancholy man? But I was sure of it.

My father certainly went out of his way not to spoil us – so did my mother – and to discourage me in particular from acting in any but a manly way. Once I remarked that a little dog we had seen was sweet. He made a face, and said that I must not use that word: I should say 'nice'. I was duly careful to say 'nice' in future but I thought him unnecessarily censorious. On another occasion he found me reading my mother's copy of *The Queen*, a fashion magazine, and told me that at my age I should be reading about pirates. I thought this highly unfair. I was all for pirates, but why shouldn't I enjoy looking at the elegant ladies in *The Queen* as well?

There was no sandy beach at Littlestone, which meant we had the foreshore at low tide largely to ourselves, if we wanted it. There were sometimes a couple of bait diggers trudging over the flat bright wastes in the far distance. They wore dark thigh boots which as a child I rather envied, as an asset to the personality rather than a practical measure against the black sticky mud. I liked the mud and its marine smell; in summer I used to wander through it barefooted for miles, occasionally disturbing the small flat fish who lay waiting in the ooze for the sea to return. I was not aware of the weaver-fish, with its highly poisonous spines whose poison can cause acute agony, even death when untreated. The wife of Field Marshal Montgomery is thought to have died in this way, after paddling with her children off the east coast. The victor of Alamein was then an unknown major. He is reported never to have mentioned her name again, and never looked at another woman.

I was fortunately ignorant of the weaver-fish and of Montgomery too, naturally enough, although I was devoted to Hannibal, whom I read about in Warne's *Encyclopedia of Pictorial Knowledge*. A vigorous drawing showed him surveying Italy from the Alps, his famished men beside him with their short swords drawn. At Cannae in another picture Roman legionnaires were desperately defending themselves against the Carthaginian troopers pressing down on them. I was bitterly disappointed when Hannibal lost the war, but by the time I was seven and a half I had left behind both the Carthaginians and the pleasures of our muddy foreshore. I struck off inland, to the golf links and the mysteries of the marsh. And to Dr Syn of course.

The links was not only a haunt of mystery and romance, where smugglers and owls made their homes in deserted cottages. It was also a social setting, a place of sophistication, and fascinating new enigmas. From its edges I could observe the local gentry at play, recognising some as neighbours and acquaintances, and speculating to myself about those whom I could not identify. Breasting the bright skyline with their golfbags, sometimes with a caddie or two in attendance, they had a heroic look which I took for granted: it was their promise of sophistication which intrigued me more. Most of them wore plus-fours and suede leather jackets.

Our family had these too; even I had one, a present from my mother on my last birthday. But it had only buttons down the front, not a zip. Zips, less common then than now, were for me an essential mark of sophistication and maturity. My brothers had them; so did my mother, whose golf jacket would have suited Papagena in *The Magic Flute*, Maid Marian on a romp with Robin Hood. Its soft, very dark green suede had a woollen edge of the same hue, and the zip fastener was ornamented with a spray of dark green leather tassels. I loved it, studied and relished its every detail, and felt proud of my mother when she was wearing it. I felt she was the equal of any lady on the course, even the dashing Mrs Bruce, whose family lived in a great red castle of a house further down the sea-wall, and who had written a novel which my mother had taken out of Boots' library. It was called *Duck's Back*.

[29]

My mother explained to me how clever the title was. 'Like water off a duck's back', she told me, was a proverb. It meant something one could take in one's stride, as the heroine of the novel did when she fell in love. I felt sure that this heroine was none other than Mrs Bruce herself, but in spite of my new devotion to the sophisticated world I felt no urge to read *Duck's Back*. I opened it but found the sentences incomprehensible and unseductive. My mother said loyally that it was clever, but I felt something was missing none the less. I plunged thankfully back into the world of *Dr Syn*.

Familiar and unfamiliar figures on the links could be watched from the top of the sea-wall, where the concrete curve and the line of houses behind it came to an end. It was here, where tall plumy reeds made a jungle between the drainage dykes, that it occurred to me to make a secret lair for myself, from which I could survey all that took place on the links.

I decided it should be tunnelled into the marram grass and sandhills like a large rabbit burrow. It does not seem to have occurred to me that once inside my burrow I should not have been able to see anything at all. Perhaps that was the real point: perhaps I really preferred not to see anything, and only supposed, in a notional way, that it would be a fine idea to watch the traffic on the links.

The first morning I managed to make only a feeble scrape in the sand. Then it occurred to me to confide in Michael. At first he was only amused and superior, but when I showed him the place he began, as I hoped, to view the project as a challenge, and he determined to make it a practical proposition. With me keeping guard and watching admiringly he soon disappeared underground. I crept in after him to help remove the excavated sand, and by lunchtime we were both invisible.

It was dark and cramped in the tunnel. After the first thrill there seemed nothing much to do, and I began to wonder if all romantic prospects ended in this sort of monotony, even though there were moments of undoubted excitement when we heard almost over our heads the voices of passing golfers, sounding muffled and hollow.

Having completed his work Michael lost interest. He had the good sense to order me never to go underground by myself, but he need hardly have bothered. I had enjoyed the enterprise in his company, but it had had the effect of inhibiting my own daydreams. The best place for the tunnel was in bed at night, when I drew up my plans in my mind, full of secret store rooms lined with tins of sardines and kegs of spirit (whatever they were: they featured lavishly in *Dr Syn*). I installed a ventilation shaft or two. In the daytime I attempted to draw a cross-section of the workings, ornamented with grass on the top and a lark up in the sky. Michael smiled wearily when I showed it to him, and indeed it was a disappointing affair compared to my daydreams in bed, when I had magnified the golfers' voices into the guttural conversation of German officers – the villains from whom we were escaping.

I disobeyed Michael's orders a day or two later, just to confirm that the real thing bore little relation to what I had been dreaming about. I was too timid to do more than just submerge, and as I returned to the surface a voice addressed me. 'Good evening,' it said, as if I were a fellow grown-up encountered at the club.

The speaker was Major Bucknall, a gaunt, courteous relic of the war, who lived by himself in one of the coastguard cottages. Like some solitary nocturnal bird he only appeared on the links in the evening, playing a few holes by himself, the holes that were furthest away on the course. I often saw him in the far distance, stalking quietly along in the golden evening light. There was something comforting and inspiring about his distant figure, but he was also an intimation to me of that unknown excitement in the lives of others, the people of the links, indeed all the denizens of Littlestone, except ourselves.

And here he was, actually addressing me. Overcome by my stammer I could manage only a faint gargling sound in reply. But waving his hand in courteous farewell the major was already striding away over the dusky turf.

Something in me determined on the spot to be more sociable in the future. I would dig no more lairs for myself, even with Michael's help. And when I passed close to people, on the links or elsewhere, I would incline my head a little and say to them, 'Good morning,' or 'Good evening,' as the case might be.

The chance was soon given to me to put this resolve into practice. Adjacent to the main links was a nine-hole course for ladies. My brothers despised it, but my mother was not above putting in an occasional practice round, with me carrying her slender bag of clubs.

On these occasions she would urge me gently to try a

few shots myself. I was nearly nine now, and if I were to play golf – and she hoped I would, because there was a lot of fun to be got out of it – I ought to start as soon as possible. To this well-meant encouragement I returned an evasive reply. I knew I would much rather take part in the game as a spectator only, an enthusiastic auxiliary. Once I began to try to hit the ball everything would be different, and I would be vulnerable to all sorts of criticism and advice which, however well-meaning, would destroy my pleasure in the links itself, and what went on there. I think my mother understood this feeling in her own way, because she never bothered me for long. She went on playing in her own quiet absorbed style – she was not very good at it – while I marked her card at the end of every hole, and fulsomely praised her occasional good shots.

Although one was discouraged from doing either, it was much easier for a small boy to wander by himself on the ladies' course – naturally keeping well away from the fairways – than among the spacious and intimidating perspectives where men strove to shorten the long ninth with a really good drive, or carry the cross bunker at the famous fourteenth. Even my brothers could not yet manage some of these things, though they were in a fair way to do so. Apart from the indignant cries of 'Fore' which would have greeted any trespassing into the path of the players on the main course, I was frightened of the balls themselves, which could suddenly appear out of the wide sky to pitch soundlessly along the turf. To be in the line of fire would be to court disaster.

When on my own, therefore, I was careful only to

potter warily in the distant rough of the 'Ladies', with
the excuse if I was ever challenged of looking for a lost
ball, perhaps one my mother had failed to find a day or
two previously. I became good at finding lost balls. It
was rare to discover a nearly new one, and if I did I
presented it jointly to my brothers, with all the pleasure
of a generous donor.

It gave me intense satisfaction when they acknowledged the gift with real pleasure; new golf balls were
expensive things, and a find in premier condition was
well worth having. Old ones a good deal cut about I
quietly reserved for myself, for no very good reason
except the pleasure of having a secret hoard. I hid a
clutch of them in the warm sand among the dunes,
like crocodiles' eggs as I imagined, remembering also
the she-cobra guarding her eggs in the *Jungle Book*.

I had another reason for exploring the distant rough on
the 'Ladies'. My ruined cottage was itself not far away,
but nearer at hand were one or two deep dark pools,
lying at the extreme edge of the rough. No life seemed to
stir in those stagnant salty depths, probably linked with
the sluices that ran into the sea. But there was a copy
of Wordsworth's poems at home, and leafing through
its totally uninteresting and barren pages I found some
lines about a pool frequented by leeches. Interest was at
once aroused. What were leeches? There were sometimes
'leech-haunted swamps' in the adventure stories I had
read, but that these creatures – whatever they were –
should actually be discoverable in England gave me a
new idea.

I had often lain on my stomach looking down into the

black salty water of the little pools, and now I could do so with a new interest. I probed their depths with an old wooden club Michael had outgrown and casually bestowed on me. I loved it. The dark hickory shaft was beautifully stippled by frequent oilings, and I greatly preferred such clubs to the steel-shafted ones now in favour, shiny and elegant as these might look in the display cases of the Professional's shop.

I was doing this one day, still disappointed of any sign of the sleek black and sticky creatures I supposed leeches to be, when the head of my ancient club struck something round and solid. The pool was deep, but I patiently manoeuvred the object, until I could reach in an arm well above the elbow and secure it. Disappointment. Not a leech or the skeleton of a leech, as I hoped it might be. Only a golf ball – but a perfect one. It was a Dunlop 65, the best brand and, as I saw when I had dried it on my handkerchief, totally unmarked. Its first shot into the air must have been its last. Wildly mis-hit, no doubt by some eccentric but powerful lady, it must have soared out above the lefthand rough – a truly heroic case of 'slicing' – and plunged, as it must have seemed for ever, into the dark depths of my pool. I put it in my pocket, well satisfied.

As I rolled over to get up I found I was not alone. A tall young man was gazing down at me. To me, lying on my back and dazzled by the sun, he seemed a giant whose shape blocked out the entire skyline. How long had he been there? I devoutly hoped he had not seen me find and pocket the brand-new golf ball.

Here was the chance to practise my new social ideas.

I remembered the 'Good evening' which Major Bucknall had so effortlessly uttered when he happened to surprise me emerging from my sandy underground lair. Suppose, before rising to my feet, I were to give this apparition a cool but cordial 'Good morning'? An excellent idea, except that I could not find my tongue, or any way of getting out the words. Instead I scrambled to my feet with undignified haste. The person confronting me was not so enormously tall after all when I was at the same level. He looked about my eldest brother's age.

But there was something indefinably different about him. For one thing he wore no suede jacket, no stockings and plus-fours. In spite of his apparent age he had on a pair of sandy-coloured shorts and a faded pink blazer with a badge on the pocket. To wear one's school blazer in the 'hols' would in our circles be considered a solecism too gross even for overt sneers. This young person would be simply ignored, not visible. It was in the light of this knowledge that I suddenly felt quite at home with him, although my natural instinct was to shrink away from anyone of my own age and kind who looked in my direction.

Whistling to himself he peered down into the pond, in which nothing now revealed itself beyond muddied water. Contrary to all my resolutions I was still speechless. But he broke the social ice with an unexpected remark.

'Have you ever seen a heron's skull?' he asked. 'I've got one at home.'

Looking into the water he seemed again to muse, unaware of me.

'A heron's skull,' I murmured, lost in the contemplation of what such an object must be like. Leeches were nothing to this. I saw the huge delicate eye-sockets (I knew from my bird book that the eyes of a predator could be as much as a fifth of its total weight), the long straight yellow beak, like a spear . . .

'I could show it to you, if you like,' he went on with the same abstracted manner as before, as if he hardly knew what he was saying. But I noticed his eyes were now focused on mine, and as sharp as I imagined the heron's to be.

Suddenly I remembered a phrase from a book, a historical romance, which had caught my fancy for some reason. Probably one by the then popular author, Stanley J. Weymer. A cunning old gentleman, encountering the stalwart young hero at an inn, had inquired coyly: 'If it be a proper question, who are you?' The words were the author's, not mine, and this seemed an appropriate moment to try them out.

'Excuse me,' I observed, 'coyly' I hoped, although I was not quite sure what the word meant. 'If it be a proper question, who are you?'

For a moment the blue eyes looked amazed, absolutely astounded. The boy clearly could not believe what he had just heard. I was in a bit of a panic myself. Perhaps the phrase I had used was incorrect today? Out of place? Or just downright rude?

Suddenly he burst out laughing. 'If it be a proper question?' he repeated incredulously. No doubt it was the use of the subjunctive that struck him as comic, though at the time I had no idea what the subjunctive was.

His amusement greatly relieved me. Indeed I began to feel rather pleased with myself, as children do when they succeed in making the grown-ups laugh. For part of my relief was the sudden realisation that here was not a boy at all, whether of my brothers' age or older. Here was not a boy at all but a man; and I much preferred men, grown-ups of any kind, to boys.

He seemed to realise that the game was up. That was a conclusion that I reached years later on, naturally; but even at the time I had the exhilarating sense of having won something: a game, a competition.

'If it be a proper question?' he repeated again. 'Well, I don't know whether it is or not, but my name is Peter Russell.' He made no further reference to herons' skulls, or showing his particular specimen to me.

'Peter Russell.' The name had at once had for me a singular enchantment. Somehow none of my acquaintances had a name in the least like that. And I repeated it aloud in fascination, just as he had repeated my own question.

The man was looking at me quizzically. But at the same time he seemed to have lost interest.

I'm sure that he did have a heron's skull, and that he would have shown it to me. What else might have happened I of course had no idea at the time. In those days children – children at least of our class and background – were not warned against the possible consequences of speaking to strangers.

'Perhaps we may meet again,' he said, but not at all hopefully, as if such a further encounter were now extremely unlikely to take place.

To this I enthusiastically assented, and was going on to ask more questions and volunteer further information, since I felt that the social ice had now been well and truly broken. But to my disappointment he was already walking swiftly away, not in the direction of the golf course and clubhouse, but across the marsh towards the distant village. I gazed after him, but not with any undue sense of loss, or of being abruptly abandoned. I felt that I now possessed him in some way. He was Peter Russell, and I said the words over to myself as I walked slowly home, with the new golf ball in my pocket.

The other day I found myself wondering if it had been his real name. He might have been a local man, or possibly a schoolmaster on holiday, staying in the village. I never mentioned his existence to my parents or brothers. I felt instinctively that they would disapprove, but apart from that I wanted to keep this Peter Russell person to myself, among my other secret possessions.

The new golf ball was definitely not one of these. As I made my usual slightly furtive way home I was already anticipating the moment when I would present it to Michael and David. Its extreme newness and beauty would excite even their admiration, although I knew from experience that their thanks and praise would be more or less perfunctory. They would probably not even bother to inquire where I had found it, and that would be a good thing, as I had no wish to reveal the existence of my pool, or the heron's skull, or of course Peter Russell.

Children with my background – the upper class as

it then thought itself – at that time developed a class sense very early. I had known at once that Peter Russell was in some sense a 'gent' – one of us – even though he did not easily fit into any of the categories of our neighbours by the sea. If he was a schoolmaster, which I incline to believe, he may well have known all about the subjunctive. But why should its unexpected use by me have dissuaded him from whatever project he had in mind: possibly a not so very alarming or repellent one? Perhaps just because it was so unexpected? Having, so to speak, got to know me in this way, he could no longer regard me as a mere object of desire, as he may have done when he saw me lying on my stomach by the pool. He may have thought I was a village boy, or 'oik' as my brothers used to refer to them. I would have been distinctly flattered if he had, for although I automatically subscribed to all the class conventions in which I had been brought up, I also longed to be different. In any way, even a class way.

I never expected to see Peter Russell again, though I thought about him and his name with pleasure for some days afterwards.

Everyone at Littlestone – that is to say all the 'gents' and their ladies – played golf; and that to me was a reassurance and a comfort, even though I had no wish to do it myself. I loved so much everything that went with the game; and in late June and July that included the wild flowers growing on the edges of the links. I found out their names from Edward Step's three-volume work, which I had asked for as the present on my eighth birthday. I think my mother was in two minds about this request but she bought the book for me anyway. Cinquefoil, Ladies' Bedstraw, Houndstongue, the tall spiky blue Viper's Bugloss, which grew in the remote rough into which even golfers whose handicap was 'scratch' occasionally hooked or sliced their shots.

I had no interest in gathering specimens, examining or cataloguing them. I liked their names. The later use of herbicides means that few if any survive today, possibly only the beautiful and indestructible Evening Primrose, which grew in a stony gully by the sea, and on the sandhills where we had made the tunnel. I had occasionally picked one or two and given them to my mother, but the pale yellow that was so right in the corners of the bleached links looked washed-out and faded in her bedroom water jug; and the thin petals only seemed to last indoors for an hour or two.

In addition to all these auxiliary and concomitant things I loved Golf, the Platonic Form or idea of it. This almost religious devotion, coupled with an unwillingness to participate in practical worship, must have baffled my parents. But by the family standards of that age and culture both my mother and father were tolerant: they wisely preferred not to encourage any lack of conformity by commenting on it, although my father did occasionally grumble, as he had done at my reluctance to earn his pound note by struggling to shore from the raft.

After finishing their morning game the golfing community used to foregather in the Mixed Room, a modern extension of a clubhouse built in Edwardian times. There was also a smaller clubhouse for ladies, set modestly beside their nine-hole course, but it was seldom used.

The Mixed Room, where both sexes could congregate, was a few steps from the Pro's shop, where members kept their clubs and other belongings, with no precautions against theft in those days. At the back of the Pro's shop the caddies themselves foregathered, like labourers at a Victorian hiring fair, waiting for a job. I was rather fearful of the caddies, although they always seemed pleasant when my parents laughed and joked with them in a man-to-man sort of way. Most of them 'moonlighted', with different part-time jobs in the locality, and their sons were often boy caddies, who could be hired by ladies at half price to carry their lighter bags. Some of them were quite small and probably not much older than I was; but they were already professionals, who would give grave advice on what club to select, and take a genuine interest in their employers' game. The dashing Mrs Bruce was especially attached to one gnome-like little caddie who seemed equally devoted to her: a relationship which provoked smiles and amused comment among the other ladies.

I was more apprehensive of the boy caddies than of their fathers. The latter's movements were predictable: in the late summer evenings when the course was empty they played golf among themselves, in a serious and orderly fashion; but their children might be encountered at any hour, lurking about the course as I did myself. In such conditions they were not at all well-behaved, shouting and quarrelling among themselves and yelling derisively after me if I happened to encounter them near any of my secret haunts. Among the sand-dunes they were like wild animals who had escaped from domestic employment, and the sight of them always caused me to beat a hasty retreat.

Rather surprisingly children were permitted in the Mixed Room, or at least no questions were asked if they did not draw attention to themselves. I discreetly followed my mother in when she finished her round and was allowed a gingerbeer, which I enjoyed because I regarded it as a sophisticated drink. I sat in a corner and watched the room fill up with returning golfers until the discussion of their morning fortunes reached a crescendo. The room had a delicious indefinable smell; not just of cigarettes (mostly Turkish of course) and cocktails. It was not like the smell of any hotel or bar I have since been into. Facepowder must have come into it, and Cologne, and suede leather which had spent the morning in close proximity to energetic women wearers. All mingled with the salty fragrance of sand and sea.

It was always known as the Mixed Room, but its chief appeal for me was the women and their loud though never raucous voices, and the unrecognised scent of femininity. Diana was there with all her nymphs, and their extensive hunting equipment, their leather golfbags brown or green, some with hoods and with gaudy close-furled umbrellas clipped on to them. These things lay easily about among all the easy chairs. I sat with my gingerbeer on an upright one in the corner of the room, listening to my mother talking to Mrs Alan or another of her friends.

While waiting for my father and brothers to appear I pondered the status of Littlestone among the other courses of the Kentish coast, which I knew about only from the cards and notices of competitions displayed in the main clubhouse. Was Littlestone on a par with Rye or Deal, where friendly foursomes were sometimes played between us and them? I knew we could scarcely compete with the Royal St Mark's at Sandwich, but that, as I had often heard my father and brothers say, was in a class by itself.

I enjoyed every minute in the Mixed Room; I hoped my father and brothers would be some time coming. I might even be stood another gingerbeer by Mrs Alan, whom I greatly admired. She was not dashing like Mrs Bruce, but she was tall and dark, and kind in an anxious almost excessive way. My mother, the elder by ten years or so, was fond of Mrs Alan, but also, as I now suspect, slightly patronised her: her extreme desire to please obviously lent itself to a touch of patronage.

We called her Mrs Alan because she had a son with that Christian name. Even my parents had taken to using it because her real married name was not mentioned. Her husband was in China, having deserted his family. Commonplace enough today, but in our circles at that time it was most unusual and fairly scandalous. Mrs Alan must have lived on handouts from relatives, but seemed, at least to me, as well-off as the rest of us. I had seen my father shake his head and refer to her delinquent spouse as 'no good'; and Mrs Alan's position, still officially married as she was, and with a nearly grown-up son, was clearly an anomalous one. Alan and my brothers played golf and tennis together. Although he was quite a bit older they contrived themselves to patronise him a little: I could grasp the process much more clearly in their company than I could in the case of my mother, with whom patronage took the form of kindness as careful and thoughtful as Mrs Alan's own.

Since my mother gently refused Mrs Alan's offer of another drink and would not let her buy me one either, we awaited in enforced dryness the arrival of the rest of the family. I loved the Mixed Room so much that I did not mind the absence of gingerbeer. I remembered Hannibal, and wondered what Peter Russell would look like, were he to walk in like a general about to address his troops. He would of course be wearing the helmet and armour illustrated in my book; but I had the feeling that he would none the less not go down well. The troops would not spring up as Hannibal's had done, and clash their weapons in acclamation, vowing to follow him anywhere. If the mysterious Peter Russell were not fully equipped in Carthaginian style his bare brown legs and faded blazer would cause positive embarrassment, especially when the Mixed Room saw, as I had done, that contrary to appearances he was not a boy at all but a man.

Never mind; I still felt proud of having met him, and of what I had said to him. 'If it be a proper question, who are you?' He had told me who he was, and that was all there was to it, and I should never see him again; but it gave me a secret pleasure that he was a part of my life that no one else would ever know about. Being secretly pleased with oneself is a childhood compensation for bruises to the ego almost if not quite involuntarily inflicted in the give and take of family life; and now I felt I had another private talisman to protect me from them.

The Mixed Room was filling up. The scent of drink steadily intensified, as did the hubbub of Standard English voices (except that no one then seemed to know about Standard English, or the alternatives in vogue today). I watched the barman prepare pink gins for newcomers, taking a slice of lemon peel, bruising it in his fingers and asperging it over a measure of Gordon's. In a rising scent of lemony spirit he took up the angostura bottle, shook a few drops into each glass, stirred them with a little chromium stick, and carried the tray to the seated ladies.

Most of the gentlemen preferred to get their drinks at the bar. My father and brothers had come in. They must have been playing a foursome with Alan, who accompanied them. I wondered how they had 'split up'. I suspected my father had paired off with Michael, the son with whom he felt most at home, and who although the youngest was the most competent golfer of the three. I had a bet with myself that they had won, and I hoped so, for it would have put my father – melancholy man as I thought him – in a good humour.

Sitting listening to my mother and Mrs Alan still chatting together, and watching the backs of Bayleys at the bar with young Alan, I saw with what seemed a sudden triumphant clairvoyance that Peter Russell was literally not of this world. He was not a boy like us or a man like my father, or even something betwixt and between. He belonged exclusively to myself, and to that moment at the side of the dark pool.

I felt exultant, perhaps slightly intoxicated by the fumes of pink gin. My mother and father preferred 'gimlets' – gin and lime – which I had heard my father call a 'clean drink', but at that moment nothing could have seemed cleaner than the pink scent reaching my nostrils as the ladies at the low table nearby called out 'Cheers' to one another.

Two days later I saw Peter Russell coming out of the ironmonger's shop in New Romney. It was quite a shock. So much for moments of vision. It was him in person all right, and yet of course it wasn't. Turning rapidly away I expelled his name from my mind as I had seen boys – village boys – spit out a gob of exhausted chewing gum.

That glimpse I had really did make me forget him, and it was only a day or two ago, lying in bed beside Iris, that I thought of him again. Why, I have no idea. But Littlestone and childhood, together with Iris as she now was, all seemed to dissolve and come together in the wanderings of memory.

I leaned over and kissed her, wondering with a now wholly detached amusement whether Peter Russell had wanted to kiss or caress me, that morning long ago beside the links.

3

It was time to go home to lunch. I wondered what there would be. At that time we had a Danish cook, Gerda, a surly shapeless girl to whom I was greatly attached. Gudrun, the pretty parlour-maid who wore a cherry-coloured uniform with frilled collar and apron in *café au lait*, I did not for some reason much care for, although she was always nice to me. I think Gudrun looked down on Gerda, who came from some outlandish part of Denmark while she herself was a Copenhagerin.

When Gudrun was out or otherwise engaged I enjoyed sitting with Gerda in the kitchen. Gerda's English, unlike Gudrun's, was extremely limited, although she could understand what was required in the house; possibly her command of Danish was not much better. I was fascinated by the words and pictures on the lurid covers of the magazines she had brought with her from home, all now tattered and dog-eared as if she had been spelling them out for years. I sometimes asked her to explain the story to me. She seemed to enjoy attempting this and grew quite animated. The man in one story had murdered the son of his best friend, why I could not make out. I felt the Danes must be more sinister than we were, as well as more grown-up in some way. I felt more respect as well as more fear for what went on in Gerda's awful magazines than I did even for Dr Syn and his activities.

My mother was pleased with Gudrun and the pretty way she had of changing the plates and waiting at table. I knew my mother did not care for Gerda and was surprised by the trouble she took to be nice to her. I suppose both girls had come to England to learn, and I remember my mother saying with satisfaction that they were much cheaper than English equivalents would have been. I think Gerda was fond of me in a gloomy way, and when she returned home she sent me a postcard of some dark urban building in the rain. I sent her a postcard of Buckingham Palace in return, with a message that began 'Dearest Gerda'. My father happened to see this when it lay on the hall table ready to be posted, and took me to task over it, brusquely pointing out that only my mother should be addressed as 'Dearest'. I attempted to argue that Gerda was just the dearest of possible Gerdas, but he dismissed the quibble.

He had a soft spot for Gerda's cuisine, none the less. She made a kind of Danish fish pie which my mother thought too rich, complaining of Gerda's extravagance. My father pronounced his own verdict one lunch-time. 'Say what you like about Gerda,' he remarked, 'but her fish soufflé is out of this world.' I had never heard the word soufflé before, and was much impressed by my father's style of utterance, as well as by his knowledgeability.

I was more impressed by him at such moments than fond of him. He was part of the general harassment of life, like school and other children. I wished he would give up trying to persuade me to play golf and tennis. Cricket and football I was starting to have to play at school anyway: both were just a part of the travail of that establishment, equally unpleasant and unavoidable.

My father suffered from an unplacid temperament. He enjoyed work, and in his job he now had little or no work to do. He was intensely loyal to the big concern he had been with since before the war, and never breathed a word against them when he was passed over for promotion. I think in those more upright business days the firm felt equally loyal – at any rate they never got rid of him. He had gone to the war in 1914 and married my mother in the course of it: she had been engaged to an officer who was killed. He used to say that he would have liked to stay in the army, but the company had asked for him back, and he went willingly. That was when they sent him to India to help look for oil. I was born there, as I said, but no oil was ever discovered. His employers could find no more work for him to do, so he sat on in an office in Whitehall waiting – had he but known it – for the big moment in his career, when at the outbreak of the Second World War he was put in charge of the whole London office, all the high-ups preferring to evacuate themselves to the country.

In the days before the war my father went up to London one or two days a week. Every Sunday at Littlestone, after my brothers were at boarding-school, I hoped against hope that tomorrow might be one of the days when he felt he should go to the office. It rarely was, but when he did decide to go he was much more cheerful. More usually Monday was a bad day, with my father departing sombrely after breakfast for a round of golf.

I had no pleasure from his absence because I knew he would have liked me to go with him. I knew my mother would have wanted it too, but nothing was said: it had to be my own voluntary decision. So I was silent until he had set out, and then spent the morning loitering in the sea-bare garden, pretending that the berberis which grew on the side of the house was 'Wait-a-bit' thorn. I had read how explorers in Africa had to cut their way step by step through miles of this terrifying growth, which tore their clothes and equipment to pieces. Forlornly I imitated their arduous progress in my mind, half aware that such fantasies were no longer quite suited to my age.

I would see my mother looking at me from the drawing-room window. Her resigned air caused me to move as if purposefully in the direction of the garage, where the family car lay as if moored. It was a faded old open Rolls, which my father had got for a song, as he said. If it still exists it must be worth today any number of thousands of pounds. But none of us thought much of it, not even my father. And my mother complained of the draught that blew through the celluloid side-curtains when the hood was put up in winter.

Neither the Rolls nor the big engine which made electric light appealed to me as material for the stories I could make up and tell myself. But twice a week Tom Mills the gardener came in the early morning to start the engine before doing his day in the garden. Tuesdays and Thursdays I thought of as rosy or crimson – happy days. Not only would my father have gone to London but Tom

Mills – Mr Mills to me – would be there as company as soon as I had finished breakfast. I never saw him start the engine, nor did I wish to – I felt it would be a frightening experience – but I loved watching him intently measuring the level of the acid in each massive accumulator. At least he said it was acid and I believed him, although I was surprised the first time I watched him fill up the level from a big bottle marked 'Distilled Water'. I was too polite to point out the apparent discrepancy; and I was in any case highly respectful of acid because Mr Mills had said that if you touched it accidentally it would burn right through you.

The Rolls had gone and I was glad of that. My father had driven it to Ashford station where he caught the London train. He would be back at six, but meanwhile I had the whole day in the company of Mr Mills, or of Gerda in the kitchen. My mother tolerated this arrangement. She would be playing golf in the morning with Mrs Alan, and they would probably make up a four at bridge in the afternoon. The idea of bridge gave me almost as much satisfaction as that of golf. I was usually allowed to sit in a corner of the room where it was going on. I decided that if I were playing I would ask to be 'dummy' the whole time. The fortunate person in that position could enjoy the game without the appalling intellectual strain of deciding what to bid and how to accommodate a partner. Though surprised and rather shocked by it I was familiar with the uninhibited sharpness with which persons always smooth and polite in normal society were privileged by the game to turn on a partner who had apparently let them down.

My father disliked bridge, and yet had no choice but to play if he were needed. He would say 'no bid' in a testy apprehensive tone, his eyes glued to the cards he held in his hand. I was intensely proud of my mother's skill at the game, and of the fact that she sometimes won as much as half a crown at one of her bridge sessions. If not present I looked forward to asking her how she had got on. I was aware of the superiority of 'contract' bridge over the old fashioned 'auction'; and I concluded that some neighbours along the sea-wall were not up to much when I heard my mother say they only played auction. My father, to whom she made the remark, merely raised his eyebrows in a quizzical way as if auction would be quite good enough for him, if he had to play at all.

All this was during an idyllic interlude. Childhood ailments, which I no doubt unconsciously welcomed, had got me off going to school, a day school near our flat in Queen's Gate. After the flat had been sold during one of my parents' bursts of economy (Gudrun disappeared at the same time and I imagine for the same reason) I was allowed to stay at Littlestone until the winter term should begin at the school which had swallowed up my brothers. David had left it for public school and Michael was about to follow. Strangers to me now – even Michael was more or less a stranger – they reappeared at the beginning of the holidays in their grey tweed suits, and showed no sign of becoming themselves again during the short weeks of the old familiarity which followed.

I did not mind. I had regressed into an earlier and solitary phase of childhood in which I went back to throwing pebbles on the beach at forts constructed of seaweed and driftwood. I trotted about after the godlike Mr Mills whom I still never addressed as 'Tom', as my father and brothers did; and on Millsless days I explored imaginary jungles in the garden, among the meagre tamarisks and euonymus stunted by the salt spray of winter gales.

Even Gerda may have noticed that I was growing backwards – I must have seemed a more precocious child when she arrived – and if so she connived in the process in her own stolid and secretive way. It may have comforted her to have a fellow-creature in a foreign country with whom she could feel on equal terms. Mrs Mills, who sometimes appeared in the kitchen and bossed Gerda around, as I imagine she must also have bossed her husband, was a person I did not care for at all.

But there was another bond between Gerda and me, although we never spoke of it, and I myself never even thought about it at the time, at least not in the way that I had once brooded for a couple of days over the phenomenon of Peter Russell. Gerda had a bleak room at the top of the house, which during this period I used to visit in the daytime. She sat there when she wasn't in the kitchen, sometimes poring over one of her dog-eared magazines but more often looking dully out over the links – her room faced away from the sea – and at the small figures scattered over its sunlit expanse.

Once, to my surprise, I found her in bed. Grown-ups never went to bed in the daytime, although it was one of my own pleasures when I was ill, or pretending to be ill, and I gazed at her with a new respect as she lay passive, staring at the ceiling. She was fully dressed as usual, in her slatternly green overall, which had made such a contrast with Gudrun's spick and span uniform of cherry serge.

Abruptly she raised her suety arms as if in invitation, and I saw tears glistening at the edges of her eyes, which looked half buried in the fat of her cheeks. I was not at all bothered by her crying, though I had been deeply embarrassed once when I came on my mother shedding a few tears in the drawing-room. My mother had hastily blown her nose and spoken to me in an irritated way – a rare thing for her. I knew she knew she should not have been doing it – such demonstrations either of grief or happiness were not the thing at all – and so I was not upset by her crossness, feeling that we had been, as it were, caught out together, and that we must both do better in future. But Danes were obviously a different matter. Being foreigners they were allowed to do what they liked, at least in the context of the emotions.

Intrigued none the less by Gerda's tears I approached the bed and was not at all startled to find myself enfolded in her arms. Indeed I was rather gratified by being given the honour of participating in this unusual Danish practice, so different from anything we did ourselves. I soon got tired of the feel of the embrace however, and Gerda was decidedly niffy under the arms. To children all grown-ups smell, or at least did in those days – either fascinatingly or disagreeably. Women smelt of scent and face-powder, men of tobacco, even if there were no other odours around.

When I wriggled away as politely as I could Gerda

dropped her arms apathetically and seemed to feel that nothing of interest had happened – which pleased me too. Denmark-wise, tears and embraces were obviously just routine stuff, like watching her roll pastry in the kitchen, or listening to her stumbling translation of one of her magazines.

Going up to Gerda's room was a positive pleasure now, none the less, and I took to running up there in my pyjamas when I was supposed to be asleep. I knew by instinct that my parents would disapprove, and I always made sure they were still safely in the drawing-room, my mother knitting and my father reading *The Times* and smoking his pipe. Gerda would be sitting on the wooden chair in her bedroom, sometimes brushing her hair but more often just gazing apathetically out of the window. She never drew the curtains, perhaps because punctually every minute there was a swift rhythmic lightening in the dark sky, from the beam of the lighthouse on Dungeness.

It seemed to hypnotise Gerda, who sat on in a sort of trance, as if the fact of being alive was a puzzle she had never even begun to understand. She would be wearing a long shapeless garment with a floral pattern, but it never occurred to me that this was what she went to bed in. I did not think of her or Gudrun as going to bed at all, in the sense that I and my family did: taking off our shoes and clothes, washing (or not, mostly, in my case), donning our pyjamas. The Danish maids were just there, day by day, like two dolls of very different appearance, and always in their dolls' costume.

One evening, after I had been pottering around her

room like a small rodent, Gerda suddenly said in her flat thick voice, 'I want to feel what man be in bed. Come in bed here.' She said this with the same apathy and lack of interest with which she let me flour the pastry dough (my father was partial to pastry) or asked me by gestures to turn the handle while she fed the mincing machine. I received her suggestion in the same spirit. She held back the sheet, gestured me to get in, and followed. She lay on her back, staring at the ceiling; she didn't look at me or show awareness of my presence. We were a close fit and I was crammed against the wall as if in a game of sardines. I might have been lying beside a big dead fish, a whale or crocodile.

It soon began to feel very uncomfortable; but I was resolved to endure it for the sake of politeness, and showing that I could be as good as a Dane in carrying out this to us unusual practice. But I did think how very boring it was, and how unlike my usual pleasure at being in my bed and reading a book or *Wings* magazine. Perhaps Gerda found it boring and uncomfortable too, because to my relief she soon rolled out and released me. I said good-night and crept down to my own bed, a delightful place by contrast.

Going to real school seemed the end of the world. It certainly was the end of that last childish period, into which I had gone thankfully backwards into the past, in the knowledge that the future was none the less certain to come. When at last it came, and I was going off to school next day, there was no question of keeping, as I knew I ought to do, a stiff upper lip.

The full horror of it came over me when I went to bed, curling up small and as it felt for the last time. I had no heart to read a book. I slept at last but then I woke, and started helplessly to cry. Almost at once my mother came in: I think she must have been expecting it. It seemed a dreadful omen of what must be coming that there were no reproaches, no tacit disapproval. All such conventions seemed beside the point, as if I was to be hanged tomorrow. My mother took me in her arms, cradled and shushed me. I stopped crying at once, appalled at this disquieting kindness, and embarrassed by it too. I found she was saying, 'You must see the new moon, darling, but not through glass. I'll put the window wide. And then you must kiss your hand to it seven times and wish.'

With her arm round me I stood at the window, still snuffling back tears, and obediently went through this unfamiliar ritual, as outlandish as the Danish habit of going to bed in the daytime. She had never mentioned it before, just as I could not remember her ever calling me 'Darling' before. It occurred to me that there must be modes of behaviour even in England which were still unknown to me. Rather like those unusual things that were done among the Danes.

'Have you wished?' said my mother. I hadn't, but I nodded dumbly. 'Then back to bed and go fast asleep,' she said, with a return to something like her usual briskness, 'and in the morning it will be quite all right.'

Next day came, naturally enough, and my mother wasn't far wrong. I found it easy, when the moment came, to seem composed, and to be properly indifferent. I was lucky too. My brother Michael, who had just finished his last term at the school, had volunteered to escort me on the train journey and show me where things were and what to do. As an illustrious old boy his commanding presence would lend me, as a new boy, the glamour of the connection: I would not begin entirely raw and unknown, with a personality to make out of nothing. I should be Bayley *Mi* or *Min*, the direct heir of the distinguished couple who had gone before me.

I was sensible, too, of the sacrifice Michael was making on my behalf, and guilty about it, for it was his last day before going off to his new school, and he would otherwise have spent it in some preferred favourite activity, probably at least two rounds of golf. But nothing was said of this sacrifice, and in face of such silent generosity I could only do the decent thing myself, departing in the comfort of his company with as near an imitation of the Spartan boy as I could manage.

This precluded any leavetaking of Gerda, and fortunately it was not one of Mills's days. I was conscious that if I went into the kitchen I should break down, and once the bonds of stoicism were snapped anything might happen. It was the thought of leaving Gerda and the kitchen that had most oppressed me in the night, and it did not strike me that for Gerda herself my going away might be a matter of complete indifference. In fact as I passed the kitchen door on my way to what I thought of as execution I caught a glimpse of Gerda doing something at the table and waved what I hoped was a nonchalant hand. She did not look up or seem aware of me and this in some odd way cheered me very much. By the time we were in the car, my mother driving, and going to the station, I felt ready for anything, and began questioning Michael with animation about how to comport myself at school. He looked surprised; for he had already taken trouble to initiate me in what and what not to do, but like everyone else, as it seemed, that morning, he made no comment.

I never saw Gerda again. When I came home at the end of term she was gone, and I asked no questions. With her went my childhood. Littlestone itself never felt quite the same.

4

This feast of memory seems never to have existed for me, before these days when Iris has lost her own memory. Or so it seems to me today, when I lie in bed and luxuriate in thoughts about Gerda and Littlestone and times past, memories which have been brought to me, as if with the flourish of a *maître d'hotel*, by one of Dr A's closest friends and allies. The friend who ministers to her, as she lies beside me, is not recollection but unconsciousness, the tranquil shallow doze in which she will lie, I hope, for two hours yet, murmuring and crooning a little at intervals.

Might she herself be soothed at these times of the day by some obscure knowledge of the compensatory pleasures which memory, let loose now like a horse in a meadow, is bringing me? It seems possible: or do I just like to think it might be so? Remembering for love of doing it – a comfort food – is bound to be selfish. But selfishness can itself help the very person who might seem cut off by it. The comfort I give Iris depends on my ability to lead this inner life, whose vividness ironically depends on Iris not being present in it. It is all pre-Iris; all done and gone long before our own life together.

So I return to Gerda, as if stretching out my own

arms this time. Permissible to feel that Gerda, if she still exists, could only be pleased by being the focus of such recollection. At least I should like to think that someone of that time, whom I hardly remember, might none the less be remembering me. I think – I almost hope indeed – that Gerda may have forgotten me utterly. That would give greater intensity to my own present sense of her.

Would it be perverse to say we only want to remain alive in the memories of those we have ourselves forgotten? But if Gerda is married, and a grandmother, living in a small Danish town, shrunken and white-haired perhaps, or still fat and uncouth, I do not want to know about it – to think about it rather. Perhaps she became a girl of the streets in Copenhagen (yet I feel that I know, in some way, that she would never be anything less than respectable). Perhaps a sodden *plongeuse* in some seedy provincial hotel? Or perhaps she returned to England, her conquest of the language miraculously complete, and settled down here? A much valued cook-housekeeper, in some family that loved her and her fish soufflé, and continued to cherish her when she was old and grey?

But all this means nothing. Gerda is not there. Only in my mind. The mind that is helped and solaced by the same demons, the same friends, who have destroyed the mind of an Iris who is close to me now, closer to me than ever, and yet far away.

Walking in a dream, with Iris beside me. And thinking of Gerda and the kitchen, the links in the distant sea air, the figures far away on it, trudging purposefully along.

*   *   *

They come and go on these walks. I can't hold them long in my mind. Perhaps because Iris, on our slow routine walk, is herself a soothing presence. In the house she is a constant source of anxiety, for herself and for me. But once out, and moving slowly along, we become a couple in harmony, like the nearly blind lady whom we sometimes meet, and her guide dog. The dog, a plump placid retriever, ambles quietly at his mistress's pace, and seems happiest to do this, though his own native instinct must be to tear about at top speed, investigating this and that, sniffing lamp-posts and excreta. I too should like to walk at top speed – I couldn't run now – anywhere, as far away as possible.

Well, so would Iris. When I have forgotten to lock the door and she has got out she can cover the ground very quickly at her determined shuffle. Her impulse then is not exactly to escape, only to get away. We share it. And that makes it all the easier to amble along together, comforting each other by our presences. Iris starts to speak, does not get very far, but it does not seem to worry her out here, in the deadly familiarity of the North Oxford street. I too start to say things to her which do not get very far. They glide gently underground, or into the air, and are lost in our mutual vacancy, and in that growing familiarity of my conscious being with childhood's daydream world. Second childhood? A parallel to the world of poor Iris?

There is no desperation now in either of us, though we have plenty of it at home. It was probably in my mind the other day when I found myself starting to hum some Schubert. *Winterreise* had been on the radio a day or two before, and the singer had given great vigour to my favourite lines.

> *Nun weiter denn, nur weiter,*
> *Mein treuer Wanderstab! . . .*

I am not mad about *Winterreise*, really preferring the more comfortable sentimentality of *Die Schöne Müllerin*. I don't go for the old *Leiermann* at the end, the *Wunderlicher Alter* who seems to be about to act the part of a Holy Fool to the mad and distracted young man. My favourite bit is the wild triumphant strain of *Nun weiter denn, nur weiter*, as he gives way to his impulse to go on, go farther, anywhere, anywhere to escape the madness in his mind. This must be why Iris stands at the front door, rattling the handle. Anywhere, anywhere, to get out of it all.

As we wander along, 'intellectual being' begins to play with ways of translating the lines. 'Further now, still further, my good walking stick'? Doesn't sound the same somehow, naturally enough. 'My trusty *wanderstaff*'? There's a touch of the German magic in that perhaps, although it's magic of a comical kind.

Anything will do to think about, to wonder about. Anything at all. Sometimes I babble out such a fantasy to Iris, as if in response to the anxiety-fed beginnings she seems to be telling to me. But there is no sign of recognition now. There used to be the ghost of a polite smile. He is saying something silly, bless him. I don't get it, but I shall humour him by pretending to do so. That's what it looked like once, but not any longer.

Is it the absence of any such goings-on now in Iris's

mind which stimulates the production of them in my own? As if my own brain chemistry were responding to a deficiency in another brain, involuntarily seeking to compensate? All such ways of looking at it are probably equally misleading: anything looked at in the mind vanishes by the act of looking? A kind of Heisenberg effect?

These little walks round the block together. Without them now I don't know what I should do, and I never want them to end, and to have to go inside again with Iris. I know she feels the same reluctance, but she doesn't seem to know what it is, what causes it. For me it is like two prisoners going back to their cell after a permitted period of exercise together.

After the *Winterreise* hero and his walking stick I start to think this morning about Jackson, the mysterious hero of Iris's last novel. Perhaps because of what was about to happen she was much more forthcoming to me about this novel than she usually was about work in progress. In fact I remember that her forthcomingness made me vaguely uneasy. A bad sign? She only thought of calling it *Jackson's Dilemma* when it was virtually finished; before that it had been just *Jackson*.

His dilemma may be the plot of the book, but who was Jackson? She said she didn't know: she was puzzled by him. It seems obvious today – perhaps too obvious? – that in one sense at least he was what was coming. The dark foreshadow of her present disease.

Heard the owl hooting this morning, before six, when it was still quite dark and we lay in bed together. I was propped up and beginning to type: Iris not quite asleep but drowsing. She used to say she liked the sound of the typewriter in the early morning. She had never used one herself, nor did she ever try to write at this hour.

Like the owl I have become a nocturnal creature. Now the hateful summer is over at last and blessed autumn properly begun, I feel at home in the early morning darkness. As I do in the late evenings, between nine and midnight. No 'work' then. If there is any sort of thriller on – an American not a British one – I am watching the television. Iris is asleep, and will sleep without a sound until I crawl into bed at one or two in the morning. Then she makes little noises, stretches, sometimes gets up. This is her good time too. Often in the next few hours she wakes me by humming. I reach over to her then and we stroke each other. If she talks much or wanders round the house it is harder to go back to sleep.

Not much sleep in the night, but I prefer it that way. I still manage to sleep deeply for an hour in the afternoon. Iris will drowse beside me then too, if she is not in one of her wanderfits, now increasingly frequent, when she carries clothes or sticks and stones about the house, or pulls again and again at the locked front door. Since I know it is locked – I sometimes used to forget when we came in from the walk round the block but now I check it carefully – I try to pay no attention. I *will* myself to sleep. But it is impossible. I lie listening to the sounds, muffled exclamations as if from the bottom of a well. '*Going – going*' sometimes, or '*Soon – help*.'

There is a story by Walter de la Mare in which an old gentleman in his country house wanders about at night saying, 'Coming, coming.' His voice is querulous but there is a dreadful patience in it. He has convinced himself – or maybe it is true? – that the house is aswarm with ghosts, who summon him all night long from every corner.

No use trying to nap away this afternoon. I get up and go down to make tea. Teatime, though it is too early for it: any appearance of routine can sometimes have a calming effect.

Iris still picks up whatever she can find on our walks round the block. Old sweet wrappings, matchsticks, cigarette-ends. She has a sharp eye, sharper than mine, but I am gazing with my own sort of fascinated attention at what is going on among the trees and in the sky. Autumn at last. And then winter. Thank goodness for both of them. The misty rain and the yellowing chestnut trees are what I seem to need. They are like the dusk and the dawn which are my hunting hours. The owl's too.

Suddenly feel happy and skip along, with Iris responding, as she always does to a jovial atmosphere. Autumn and winter are certainly good friends of ours. Does her good angel promise her that these are the last she will have to see?

Now I pat Iris vigorously on the bottom and she smiles like an angel's friend. I often tease her about being like a water-buffalo, a big creature lumbering out of the pond, always getting in the way. And it's true that at home she not so much clings to as nudges me, always just in front of me when I am trying to do something in the kitchen, or just behind if I turn round to go to get something. I think she understands the pantomime of the water-buffalo, though it seems unlikely that the word itself is still there. But she used to love the idea of water-buffalo, or pictures of them.

But the old paradox remains; indeed becomes more paradoxical than ever. I must be there; she wants me there every minute; if I am in the loo she stands outside the door. Her little mouse-cry comes up or down the stairs. And yet the wild urge to escape, *nun weiter denn, nur weiter*, seems at moments to be equally strong. When she stands by the front door rattling the latch she is quite indifferent to where I am or what I am doing.

Water-buffaloes. Nice animals. The way she moves just in front, or accidentally nudges me, seems very like an animal. Eating is becoming rather like that too. She eats best if I put the spoon to her mouth: otherwise hardly anything gets done. 'What a silly animal it is!' We laugh, and I have no trouble getting another spoonful in. Baked beans or ice-cream. Iris wouldn't mind if both came together; she might even prefer it. She eats so little now and yet she looks so well. When she is asleep I eat and drink wildly – all sorts of unsuitable things – and they make me feel as if I am wilting and vanishing, disintegrating and coming to pieces.

Sex is not exactly a friend of Dr A. It seems in any case to have more or less given us up. Iris never bothered with it very much: now not at all, and that seems natural. Only a short while ago I used to think: I don't mind sex going in fact, if it doesn't go in fancy. I used to spend long and happy hours pondering and dreaming about it.

My daydreams now are not about sex but about the women in my childhood, which seems quite a different thing. Even if it isn't.

Animals. What have they got to do with Dr A, or with his friends? Actually quite a lot. When I can see us, feel us, as two animals pushing about together, nudging and grooming each other, grunting together as they bask in a mutual doze. Our animal togetherness is better than sex, and makes me forget Iris's night conversations downstairs. I don't feel haunted any more. I don't feel like the old gentleman in the de la Mare story, in thrall to a pack of ghosts, trudging up and down flights of stairs in the small hours and calling out querulously, 'Coming – coming.'

5

The only ghosts are safely in the past. Good, good ghosts, from far away and long ago. And they were liberated by a very animal-like experience – the feel of tugging at my vest to free it from the arm of the windsor chair. I might have been pushing at Iris to get her out of the way. My fellow-animal always beside me while memory disports itself, courtesy of Dr Alzheimer.

Iris blessedly back in sleep: she has hardly woken. I am free to drowse beside her and 'think about things'. Distant things. Is it because of our present animal close-ness that no memories seem to come back of the times the two of us have spent together? Later perhaps. Does true memory require distance, space in which to uncoil itself, like a genie coming out of a bottle?

Alzheimer, the dark doctor, seems to have got hold of all memories of our life together before his time. He has wiped them, or whatever it's called, from his computer. Or he doles them out at unpredictable intervals. But he has given handsome compensation, a really lavish pay-off in terms of the pre-Iris memories which now for me enchant our walks together, our early mornings in bed.

I think of my mother shushing and cradling me, to my

extreme surprise and no little embarrassment, that night before I went to boarding-school for the first time. Even in my misery and apprehension I felt embarrassed, and she must have felt me stiffen. She relinquished me and became brisk, I remember that. Did she feel any regret that she had brought us up to be so unresponsive, so wary of her physical comfort? I ponder the matter now, when it doesn't in the least matter, and I enjoy nothing but the memory itself, devoid of regret or guilt or any emotion. And yet I am so pleased she did it; and that she once showed me the new moon.

Recall cannot be much bothered with the people at the school. Of course I can remember them, but it is hardly any fun to do so, just as there was hardly any fun in being at school. Just getting through the days. Waiting to get back to Littlestone. Our house had been sold after I had been at school for less than a year – another burst of parental economy – and from then on we led a nomadic existence, never leaving the seaside but moving progressively further down the front, from one rented flat or bungalow to another. We ended up at the point furthest from the links and nearest to Greatstone-on-Sea, a bungalow town of decidedly inferior social standing. I didn't mind that, because I had discovered an absorbing new holiday activity. Sailing my boat.

It was a crude little model of a Breton fishing lugger, with a red sail. It belonged to a boy at school called Michel, who must have been partly French though he seemed perfectly normal and indeed rather dull. I fell in love with the boat at first sight. Although I was by then familiar with the technique of swapping I felt there was no hope of acquiring such a precious object as that little boat. It must be a prestige object. So no doubt it once was, but as Michel had risen further up the school the prestige had worn off. Not, I suspect, a sensitive lad, he had none the less received intimations from his contemporaries that such things were only suitable for little boys.

To my delight and astonishment he seemed more than open to offers for his boat; although when he grasped the degree of my interest, which I found impossible to conceal, he prepared openly to drive a hard bargain. Precious as it was to him he might part with the boat, but what had I to offer? My only asset was a large quantity of 'tuck' – doled out to us twice a week under the matron's supervision. Michel was, fortunately for me, a greedy boy; and by handing over all the supplies of chocolate, 'crunchies', lollipops and sherbet which I had saved up, and even mortgaging future rations for that term and the next, I persuaded him to part with the boat at last.

From his look of satisfaction I could see he felt he had got a bargain, but my heart was filled with delirious joy. For the rest of term I hid the boat carefully in my tuck box and showed it to nobody. Then I took it home, to our latest rented accommodation, which was not far from the point where the shingly wastes of Dungeness began, a deadflat area dotted with salt pools and tracts of marsh.

My parents were tacitly apologetic, at least to my brothers, about the way we had come down in the world. They considered our gimcrack bungalow and its surroundings a dreary hole, but I loved them as much as I had once loved the links and the houses at the 'good' end of Littlestone. My brothers had other interests now, and were only fleetingly at home in the holidays. So it was by myself that I explored my new domain, and soon found a lonely lagoon which seemed perfectly adapted for the purpose of sailing my boat.

So it was, although the boat itself was not co-operative. For me she was beautiful, with her bluff bows and transom stern carved out of a single chunk of wood. During an earlier period of interests I had managed to collect most of a Player's cigarette card series called 'Curious Beaks'. I now christened my boat *Toucan*, because she looked like the big contoured beak of that tropical bird. She was a poor sailor, proceeding a trifle crabwise, but she was none the less a fine sight as she stood out from the shore with a ripple round her bluff bows. When the breeze took her in mid-pond she was apt to keel ignominiously over.

I did not mind; wrecked or upright she was always beautiful for me, and I loved her. The desolate little lagoon where I sailed her was now a place of even greater romance than the golf-links had been, or the ruined cottage. And one day, as I waited for *Toucan* to drift ashore, the scene made me remember a poem I had been fascinated by in what I already thought of as the old days, before I had been sent to boarding-school. It had been read to us by Miss Jocelyn, one of the mistresses at the day-school in Queen's Gate. I had not thought her beautiful, but she was tall, dark and mysterious, with a deep thrilling voice. The poem, 'Overheard on a Saltmarsh', was a dialogue between a goblin and a nymph who possesses a string of green glass beads. He covets them and begs her for them, but she refuses to give them up.

He had nothing to offer the nymph in exchange, I reflected, whereas to obtain *Toucan* I had fortunately possessed a whole lockerful of goodies. I had been sorry for the goblin, none the less, and thought the nymph hard-hearted, which must have been one of the perquisites of being a nymph. Saying the poem to myself brought back all its old allure, and with it came a sudden stab of real homesickness. It was my first realisation that the past is the thing, never the present, and it would be by no means my last. I thought of Miss Jocelyn, and her dark hair and thrilling voice, and the dark green velvet jacket she always seemed to be wearing. That brought back thoughts of Gerda, and how comforting her surly presence had once been. Standing by the shore, watching the capsized *Toucan* borne steadily away from me on the stiff seabreeze, I had my first true experience of nostalgia, and all its rich self-indulgent solitude.

It comes back much richer and with keener force today, as I lie in bed beside Iris and give myself up to it. Have I been given, as a kind of bonus or legacy, the memories that in her brain have been wiped away, if indeed for her such self-indulgent memories ever existed? Difficult not to feel it now as a part of a new and as it were emergency mode of consciousness. It connects with those 'short views of human life – never further than dinner or tea' which the Reverend Sydney Smith always recommended to parishioners bereaved, or in the grip of depression. I notice now that there is a positive pleasure in feeling we are getting through the time *somehow*: anyhow, as if time existed for no other purpose than to be got through.

Always something to look forward to: the coming of night and the evening drink: the time before dawn when I can give myself up to a frank enjoyment of all that's past. Anything that comes along.

An orgy of 'Wandering through eternity', as dear old Belial put it. He put it not only beautifully but accurately, for consciousness – whatever goes on inside our own head – is surely all that eternity can mean to us?

What an admirable fellow Belial sounds. Even if he wasn't very good at being a devil.

Still dreaming idly about Miss Jocelyn and my memory of her. How old would she be now – about a hundred? Less probably. She was ageless to us, but I should guess now not much over thirty. She read poetry without a poetry voice – just made it sound good. And thrilling. She did 'The Pied Piper of Hamelin' very well, but 'Overheard on a Saltmarsh' is the one I particularly remember. She sounded amused by it, and yet excited too.

Long afterwards I came on it in an anthology, and found it was by Harold Monro, a Georgian poet. He and his wife ran The Poetry Bookshop. They had tea-parties there for fellow Georgians. As a poet he had his felicitous moments, as the saltmarsh poem shows. In private he seems to have been a haunted man, a secret homosexual, with a possibly all too understanding wife. It must have been a common enough situation in those days.

Sailing my little boat slowly down the stream of memories . . . Life does seem but a dream when I can lie in bed like this, with Iris unconscious beside me, or sometimes briefly awake and making quiet little cooing or humming sounds. However bad night may have been early morning is usually a good time. At such moments we seem together, although I am feeding only on memories from the deep past long before we were married. Yet again I wonder: why am I not remembering now things we have done together? Of course there is a sense in which I do remember them; but I suppose I don't want to think about them, as I think about what happened to me, years and years ago. Will I get nauseated by such memories in time, as if by eating too many chocolates?

The present flow was certainly started by that moment when I stood trouserless in the kitchen, trying to wriggle the tail of my vest off the windsor chair. That was a kind of involuntary shock, bringing back the mantrap, the ruined cottage, the owl . . . The recall of everything else has just been deliberate self-indulgence: Gerda and the golf course, my mother showing me the new moon, the boat *Toucan*.

Had Iris been with me in the kitchen when I caught my vest on the chair I should not have had this sudden flood of memory. I should have been too conscious of her, too bothered by my own sense of her anxieties. These childhood memories are a way of escape.

We had yet another repetition of the incident this morning. Getting out of the front door is a difficulty, because Iris, in her water-buffalo guise, crowds up against me, and will hardly wait for the door to be unlocked before she is pushing through it. I have no room to shut the door, and when I do get it shut I find that the back of my coat has got stuck as it closed. I am more seriously trapped this time. When I manage to get the key back into the Yale lock it will not turn, and held fast as I am I cannot exercise any pressure. I shall have to wriggle out of the coat, like the heroine caught in the mantrap wriggling out of her dress. But no sooner is the expedient in my mind than the lock suddenly yields, the key turns and the door opens.

Iris might have escaped, leaving me standing there helpless. But no, of course she hasn't. She is herself standing vacantly, like a good water-buffalo, as if waiting for me to be beside her again, and direct her.

These repetitions, absurd as they are, give me no pleasure. Not like the first time, which unlocked memory. Once we would have joked about them together. It is a sort of joke to me now, not a specially funny one, but in the old days Iris and I would both have burst out laughing. Of course we would. Iris has in fact been watching the incident, but without any reaction. She seems to think it just something that happens every day. And I take it in the same spirit. Gravely we link arms and set out on one of our little walks. Round the block and back home.

As we go I remember a similar repetition. I once lost the lower half of my denture swimming with a pipe and mask at Lanzarote. A year or so later I did just the same thing in Lake Como. It was such an improbable misfortune that everybody laughed – our friend Audi

Villers who lives on Lanzarote, Drue Heinz with whom we were staying on Lake Como. They were sympathetic too of course, but on neither occasion did Iris laugh: she was much too concerned for me and my welfare, and she made valiant underwater efforts herself to locate the teeth. Quite hopeless in both cases. They were much too far down.

I think of her goodness about that now as we walk along. It gives me a sudden lift, and I put my arms around her, hug her, kiss her on the cheek.

As a 'carer' I am sometimes conscious of the way one ought to behave: the way, that is, in which a professional would behave. Never losing the temper, never raising the voice. Persuading and controlling in that firm wheedling tone which carers come to have. As if talking to an imbecile child. Whatever exasperations they may sometimes feel, they hide it. I don't, I can't. Hardly a day goes by without my flying into a brief frenzy, shouting at Iris, or saying in level tones something like: 'I don't know *what* to do with you – you exhaust me so much.' Or sometimes saying, with a reassuring smile, 'Have you any idea how much I hate you?'

It sounds then as if I am making a reasonable point, and she seems to receive it in the same spirit. She knows me, she wants me. She knows the violence that is in me at moments and is just controlled, but only just. When I have been struggling for minutes at a time to get arms through sleeves or heels into shoes, she can feel that surge of ungentleness very close to the surface. Once she put her hands over her head and whimpered,

'Don't hit me.' She knew better than I did what might happen.

At one level I felt horribly shocked: at another I simply accepted the possibility of what she was saying. I did want to hit her. Parents do too, I'm sure. If I'd been a parent would I have learnt more control? So useful later on, if the wife, or the husband, becomes a child again.

I could feel that Iris wasn't in the least resentful of the wish she intuited in me. Something inside her accepted it, as if it were a part of loving me and being loved. One of those tedious 'social' questions presents itself. Would a child, or a senile adult, prefer to be looked after by a parent or partner who both loved it and knocked it about? Rather than go into some sort of state care?

Depends on the degree of knocking about I suppose. The opposite of those violent impulses when I am trying to get Iris into shoes or clothes is the pleasure I find in feeding her. She hardly eats now unless I spoon it gently into her mouth. Baked beans, ice-cream. She makes crooning and glugging noises then. Highly satisfactory for both of us. No need whatever to find words and be coherent. But there was nothing in the least incoherent when she cowered, and said, 'Don't hit me.' The nearness of violence brought stark sense back into her speech.

I muse now, as we walk along, on the reasons for my reluctance to undress Iris at night. I know I ought to: it should be part of our routine. But it is such a relief to go along with her simple wish to get into bed in all her clothes, shoes included. Then I shan't have to dress her in the morning, and shan't get in such a temper with elbows and feet. The other night as she got under the duvet I said, 'You're like the Burial of Sir John Moore at Corunna, darling.

> 'He lay like a warrior taking his rest,
> With his martial cloak around him.'

Iris appeared delighted by that. Not only did she seem to remember the reference (I used to quote the poem sometimes in the old days) but she seemed pleased to think of herself as Sir John Moore, not enclosed in a 'useless coffin', but lying there in his soldier's cloak, fully dressed and ready for action, as he always slept when on campaign.

Something to think about, to amuse oneself with. And it definitely amused Iris too. We could share it. But on these little walks thoughts are usually solitary. And I no longer wonder what, if anything, is going through Iris's head. Instead I find myself coming back, full circle, like the familiar houses we shall be walking round, to the moment when I closed the front door and trapped the tail of my coat.

It was like *The Woodlanders*, the Hardy novel I now start consciously to think about. The point was, I recall, that the husband was a philanderer, as no doubt Hardy himself would secretly have liked to be. He seduces the wife of the village woodcutter – isn't she called Sukey? – as he has seduced other and grander women in the neighbourhood; and his wife finds out all about it and leaves him. The woodcutter finds out about it too, and murderous with jealousy fixes a mantrap on the woodland path the seducer (he's a doctor) uses when he goes on his professional visits.

It so happens that the doctor has just begged his wife to come back to him, and she had promised to meet him in the evening on that very path, for a discussion. Hence she is the one who sets off the trap and is nearly caught in it. In the dark the doctor finds her abandoned clothes in the jaws of the monster, and is distraught. What has happened? Is she dead?

It occurs to me now that Hardy had an unconscious recollection of *A Midsummer Night's Dream* – the play within the play. Pyramus finds Thisbe's clothes, bloodied by the lion, and kills himself. The seducer doctor of course does no such thing. The danger and escape, to say nothing of his wife in her undies, brings them back together and reconciles them. Like the wonderful and ambiguous ending of *A Midsummer Night's Dream*. Play and novel have the same woodland pastoral atmosphere. Beautiful, but disturbing.

The old Eng. Lit. again. I taught it for nearly fifty years and feel detached from it now. Glad to be so. But old habits die hard. Thinking about *The Woodlanders* has seen me through another little walk. But I really prefer my own memories.

Or do I? Those morning memories, lying in bed, are so pleasant that I took it for granted that memory could never be dull or desolate or boring. But perhaps it can? Suppose I was blind, and in a home or hospital day after day. Would memory be as good there as it is now – as comforting, as reliable? I rather think not.

Hastily think of something else. Where was I? The little

boat *Toucan*. She survived at least until the end of the war, and then must have disappeared on my parents' final move into Kent. I was still in the army in Germany at the time. But before she went to limbo, or to 'Pieland', *Toucan* made one final appearance on water.

It was after I was called up into the army, in 1943. I was on leave. Probably my first leave. We were up in London, my mother and I, and I was due to return to barracks the next day. I very much wanted to sail *Toucan* on the Round Pond in Kensington Gardens, before I went back. My mother was doubtful, but she agreed. We had *Toucan* with us in a bag. It was a fine day, nice breeze. I was just bending down in my cap, tunic and army boots to put her in the water when my mother gave a warning cry. An officer was just about to walk past us. We were supposed to salute officers. I left *Toucan* to her own devices. She sailed merrily away into the pond. I stood up and saluted. As smartly as I could.

The officer returned the salute in the normal way, and then looked at me, and saw the boat. He hesitated a moment in his stride; his expression seemed unbelieving, incredulous. He glanced towards my mother, who gave him an inviting smile. That did the trick. As if it had checked any need he may have felt to stop and investigate this unmilitary scene he looked once more from my mother to me, and then he walked on.

I breathed a sigh of relief. My mother had a fit of uncontrollable giggles. *Toucan*, having gallantly and precariously reached the middle of the pond under sail, now capsized. It would be some time before she floated in, but I knew she would come. She was the only boat on the pond that wartime day in bombed-out London. My mother and I stood waiting for her in the spring sunshine, my mother still going into a fit of giggles from time to time as she remembered the officer's face. I felt it had been a lucky escape, although I don't suppose the officer would really have put me on a charge. Presumably for slovenly behaviour while wearing His Majesty's uniform?

My father was not told of the incident. My mother and I were staying in a hotel in London that night, as a final treat for my leave before I had to go back to barracks the next day.

I wish I could tell Iris about *Toucan*. In fact I must have told her in the old days, perhaps when we visited Littlestone together. Everything now reminds me of that childhood idyll, even small things as we walk round the block together. A house under extensive repair is having metal-framed windows taken out and replaced with timber ones. Apart from the more select residences, like the one we originally had, all the seafront houses at Littlestone had 'metal casements', as John Betjeman called them. Metal was much used on smart little houses in the '30s. 'Oh the metal lantern and the white enamelled door!' Our present house has both, which I take pride in, as I do in adjacent Belbroughton Road, one section of our little walk, and celebrated by John Betjeman in his poem 'Spring in North Oxford'.

Belbroughton Road is bonny, when pinkly bursts
   the spray
Of prunus and forsythia across the public way . . .

Rachel Cecil, wife of my old friend and teacher, always used to giggle when we chanted together her own favourite lines.

> And a constant sound of flushing runneth from the
>   windows where
> The toothbrush too is airing in this new North
>   Oxford air . . .

Street and houses were new when they must have given the ebullient Betjeman his impulse to dash off the poem. Around 1927? – two years after I was born. A feeling of hope and expectation of the future at that time? I suppose it was created by reaction against the war, by the new Garden Cities, by modernity itself? All that sort of thing.

Excitement this morning. Iris escaped. After the postman came and I had to sign for something I was flurried and forgot to relock the door. A few minutes later I realised the silence. Called again and again but no reply. Overwhelming sense of being alone. But no time to think of that – rush out of the front door, look up and down the street. Nothing. Sometimes she has gone into a neighbouring garden – not hiding exactly, just out of sight.

After scouting vainly about I get out the car, drive concentrically round the neighbouring streets. No sign of her. I ring the police. A policeman in a car comes round, a nice elderly man, and says he will put out a search for her. Having taken the particulars in a leisurely

JOHN BAYLEY

way he thinks he had better just look round the house. This has happened before, so I don't point out that I have already done so. He gazes impassively at the heaps of this and that in every room. 'Most admired disorder'! – doesn't Hamlet's mother say that about the state of her son? Gertrude in the play must have meant it was something to be wondered at. But the policeman gives no sign of either wonder or admiration.

'You never know, sir,' he says. A conclusion for all occasions. Perhaps a person reported missing is sometimes found concealed and dead? Have I done in Iris and stowed her away somewhere? Why would I call the police in that case? Well, you never know.

Hours seem to pass, though actually not much more than two. The policeman sensibly advises me to stay at home. Impossible to do anything.

A loud knock on the door. I rush, and scrabble to open it. I have locked it on the inside – too late now – and for the moment can't find the key. Must have left it on the kitchen table. Run to get it, thinking distractedly of stable doors. When I've got it open there stands Iris. Expectant, sly but triumphant, enormously refreshed. She looks a bit like a schoolgirl who has won the record for running away from school the longest time. And indeed she has: she has never been away so long before.

A seraphic smile for me, and an even bigger one for the man who stands just behind her. I start to thank the man, and ask where she was found. He happened to see her – nearly at the top of the Woodstock Road. He turns to go. I thank him effusively. I am too flustered to ask how he knew it was Iris, but I manage to stutter out, 'Do just tell me your name!'

He looks amazed. 'Why I'm Valentine Cunningham, John. Your old colleague. It was just a bit of luck I happened to spot her. I'm late for a pupil – I must be going now.'

Amidst all the anxiety and relief I hadn't recognised him. My own mind must be going. I call out after him, 'I'm so sorry, Val,' and he turns and gives a wave and a smile as he gets into his car.

Iris still looks well and happy, as if basking in her achievement. How did she manage to get so far? No point in asking. I put my arms round her. We sit at the kitchen table and presently have a cup of coffee, but she hardly drinks any.

If it's warm the house cats of the area lie out on the pavement, giving an impression of the bright young people of the '20s, gossiping and showing off. Obliging animals, they always rise to have their backs stroked and rub themselves against Iris's old trousers. I point them out as we round the corner, and Iris makes little mewing noises of recognition.

In Linton Road, outside the Linton Lodge Hotel, there are always a number of interesting cars. Like all children I once loved admiring cars. There was a Hispano-Suiza at Littlestone with a windscreen which screwed up and down, and an open Mercedes with three shiny and scaly pipes coming out from its bonnet. I asked David, my eldest brother, what was the function of these pipes.

'Superchargers of course,' he said, dismissing my ignorance with kindly impatience. I had a feeling that he
might not know what a supercharger was, or what
function it performed, and so was careful not to ask
him, although I would have liked to find out more.

Today I have none of my old interest left in the
insides of cars; I don't keep up; but as part of recent
life's little compensations I like looking at them again,
especially the sleek oriental ones, with peacock logos on
their gleaming bonnets, in dark blue or purple enamel.
I have the impression that these eastern cars are washed
and cleaned with special zeal by their owners.

Our old Fiat Panda has green mould round the windows, and pigeon droppings from the trees in the front
garden under which it stands. Some delicate-looking
little seedlings – wild geranium perhaps? – are growing
in the crevice where the bonnet opens. I feel I want to
cherish them, like indoor plants.

As we shuffle along together I go on dreaming about
cars. The old Rolls at Littlestone sitting in its garage.
In the first days of our honeymoon in 1956 we visited
Littlestone on the way to Dover. We had a little green
Austin van which I had bought (it was very cheap – no
purchase tax) just before we were married, and in it we
were going to drive through France, over the Alps and
into northern Italy.

But I wanted to show Littlestone to Iris and she was
keen to see it.

The visit was not exactly a success. It was a grey day
– the weather had been awful all summer – with none
of that golden light from the wide pale-blue sky which

I remembered. The tide was far out but Iris was keen to swim, so we trudged out for half a mile across the rippled sand and mud flats. Although she waded out an immense distance Iris could only immerse herself a foot or two. I stood in the grey featureless expanse, guarding her clothes (there wasn't a soul for miles of course) and her new wedding ring which she had entrusted to me in case it should come off and be lost in the sea.

She emerged eventually, black to the knees as if she were wearing a pair of mud stockings. While she was away, becoming a small featureless figure in the grey shallows that seemed to stretch all the way to France, I had experienced a failure of nerve. Littlestone meant nothing to me now, and what else did? For the moment marriage seemed as unpromising a prospect as this mud and sky and sea. With acute nostalgia I remembered the green waves washing on the shingle and round the seaweedy groynes. It was high tide in childhood, just as the sun always shone.

I could not then share Littlestone with Iris, just as I cannot do so today, while we walk hand in hand round our unending little block. I think of it myself, as it was, and the thought inevitably separates me from her, as she now is. I loved, almost worshipped, the loneliness of childhood, the immense pleasure one felt in being alone. But that, like our marriage, was being alone among invisible but watchful angels. This is the real thing. Iris can comfort me by her presence but she cannot watch over me any more. In memory and daydream there is nothing but solitude. The friend I have come to depend on.

6

And a friend, I'm glad to say, who could well have been an enemy.

My awareness of solitude today brings back that visit to the small town of Rye, not far from Littlestone, which we made together only a few years ago. Landlocked now but once a 'Cinque Port' with the sea at its gates. The picturesque streets were garlanded for a Festival.

In his first published novel, a wonderful farrago of rusticity and melodrama called *Desperate Remedies*, the youthful Hardy observes that small towns holding 'Festivals' are the dullest things in creation. His example he calls Hocbridge, which is the real Banbury, not far from Oxford, where the proceedings are only enlivened by the heroine's father, an architect like young Hardy himself, falling to his death from the summit of the church tower.

No such excitement occurred when we were in Rye, but for me it was a memorable visit none the less. Iris, although more than willing to take part in the Festival, had excused herself from giving a talk. I would do what I could, I said, offering something on Henry James and ghost stories. From a cultural point of view James, who lived there for many years, is still patron spirit of the town of Rye.

As the easiest way of making up a little talk I brought in the other James too. This is M.R. James, sometime Provost of Eton and of King's College, Cambridge, legendary scholar and author of *Ghost Stories of an Antiquary*. One of the best of these is 'Oh Whistle and I'll Come to You, My Lad'. I had no difficulty in concocting a little 'theory' about it, which I hoped might amuse the festival-minded ladies of Rye.

The terrifying phantom of this tale, brought back to life by the note of an antique whistle, sits up suddenly in the darkness of a hotel room, feeling around, with outstretched arms of crumpled linen, for the scholarly victim in the bed. He has accidentally summoned the ghost by unearthing on the local golf course this ancient whistle or pipe and rashly blowing it.

Surely, I suggested to the Rye ladies, this apparition must be the implacable goddess of the linen cupboard, an embodiment for the author of threatening femininity? And what an appalling experience for a misogynistic bachelor, however amiable – and Monty James was certainly that – to imagine himself going snugly and safely to bed in his favourite little seaside hotel: only to wake up in the night and see a sheeted woman sit up beside him!

There were a few uncertain titters from the audience, but my little idea, such as it was, had not really struck a chord. Never mind. We were to be put up in Lamb House, Henry James's very own residence, and our kindly host and hostess, Guardians of the National Trust, gave us excellent drinks and supper. We retired to bed in good spirits – in the Master's very own bedroom.

What an honour! As we got into the comfortable double bed I wondered aloud to Iris if this was the Master's bed as well as his bedroom. Did he like to sleep in a big bed or a narrow one? Did any of the detailed and exhaustive biographies have anything to say about the matter? Iris grunted, already half asleep, and in a few seconds I was asleep too, having made a mental note to ask our host and hostess about the bed in the morning.

It must have been between three and four when I woke abruptly. There was faint daylight already in the room. Something was wrong. What was it? Indigestion, heart attack? No, I felt quite normal. Then what was the trouble?

Suddenly I realised. I felt full of an overwhelming depression, as if the day to come was to offer nothing but utter emptiness and loneliness, boredom, the knowledge of all that was lacking in life, all that had been missed.

It was so overwhelming that I could not stay in bed. I got up and went over to the window. I drew aside a corner of the thick curtain and peeped out. There, in the still grey light of dawn, was the view, unchanged, that James must have seen every morning on rising. An almost too perfect English vista of cobbled street, comfortably huddled old houses, the little church beyond. Wasn't it called Watchbell Street, an almost too perfect English name?

How reassuring it might have been for James, to look out on such a view when he got up in the morning! But somehow it did not look now as if the view had reassured him. On the contrary it had a look about it of desolation, as if it were faithfully reproducing what was in the mind

[95]

and soul of the man who had gazed out. Had it brought home that all his years had passed him by? With nothing truly suffered and enjoyed, with nothing loved?

In later years James suffered from insomnia – I remembered reading that. How many times had he looked out on that view in the summer dawn with the sensation of loneliness that I was now mysteriously experiencing? But mine had no apparent cause. On the contrary.

I crept back into bed beside Iris (James had no Iris), fell asleep at once and woke at eight feeling quite cheerful and ready for breakfast. I told Iris what I had felt when I woke in the night, or rather in the early dawn. She was sympathetic, but smiled at my suggestion that Henry James had been with us in the night. I felt sure he had. Had he been aware, or not aware, of the couple from the future who had officiously installed themselves in his chaste bedroom? There had been many others like ourselves after all, including the writer E.F. Benson who had lived in the house for many years after James's death, and who had even become the Mayor of Rye, a position James would have evaded with polished modesty and elaborate self-depreciation.

I forgot to ask our host and hostess about the bed. None the less I was privately convinced that the strange shock of waking, and then of looking out on James's motionless street, had been the only paranormal experience I have ever had. Not exactly of the occult, but of what James himself had referred to in the title of one of his last novels, *The Sense of the Past*. It had happened to be a highly uncomfortable sense. But the very acuteness of that depression made me convinced

of its authenticity – it must have come from somewhere.

It was easy after the event to start fitting the pieces
together, as it were. I had talked about the other James's
ghost story; and amused myself, if not my small audience, with notions of bachelors, fearful of women, waking
at night to see the sheets sit up in the bed, ripple into
hostile form, and seek with blind malice to envelop the
helpless male. Such a nightmare might have befallen
either of the Jameses, but of course it could not have
happened to me.

For them it was a case of things not happening, of
things which afterwards they might have longed to happen – love, passion, fulfilment. Not, in the case of both
Jameses, with a vengeful woman from the linen cupboard, but with the boy or young man of their dreams.

Fanciful no doubt. But there is no doubt too that ghost
stories can tell the truth, in their own peculiar kind of
way. In *The Turn of the Screw* James's real *donnée*, as
he would have termed it, is not the haunting of the
children but the children's own secret and inscrutable
self-sufficiency. They are of their very nature remote from
the adult world, living in a universe of their own; and
James perceives this with all the more force because for
him too the 'adult' world – love and marriage and all its
casual intimacies – were things unknown, things guessed
at, intuited, sometimes envied, never experienced.

And had I for a few seconds or minutes been inside
James's head, or his mind, when he woke in the morning
to a feeling of his life's emptiness and loneliness? Perhaps

[97]

it was presumptuous of me to feel I had; but I did feel it none the less. Perhaps if there is anything at all in the idea of 'haunting', or being haunted, it is in this sense of being slipped, involuntarily or unwillingly, into someone else's mind, someone in the past or the present.

I remembered then that other ghost story, the one by Walter de la Mare, in which the solitary old gentleman who craves for company wanders about the stairs in the middle of the night, calling out, 'Coming, coming.'

In that story the young man whom he has virtually kidnapped and forced to stay the night and be entertained at supper, wakes as I had, and finds the bedroom looking inexplicably different: looking the way a room might look to someone who was intensely afraid. The young man is not afraid; there does not at that moment seem anything to be afraid of. But then as he gets out of bed he hears voices sounding plaintively and distantly, all over the house.

I don't feel in the least depressed now as I get cautiously back into bed beside sleeping Iris, snuggle down and begin to drink my cup of tea. Freeing my tail from that windsor chair has certainly released the flood of memory. But it is easy enough to find memories when one depends on them and courts them all the time. I am conscious once more of how much they have become a way of escape; even, it must be said, a way of escape from the loved one who lies at my side. So long as I can be free to remember I can still need to be physically with her, still depend entirely on her being there.

Strange that I seemed to find myself, that time in Rye, in Henry James's mind, the mind of a man who has been dead for so many years, when I can't today imagine what it's like to be inside Iris's poor distracted head. Of course we can communicate, are in a touch so close that we both take it for granted. But it is far easier to experience, or at least to imagine, what Henry James may have felt than what Iris is, or is not, feeling.

Even while thinking that, I find myself escaping again. I am back in the Mixed Room, with the pale blue sea light flooding in, and the lemony scent of gin mingling with the suede and leather odours of coats and golfbags. Had these people really been as nice, I now wonder, as I used to be sure they were at that time, when I was seven, eight or nine years old? For me they were romance and mystery as well as casual niceness: I contemplated without envy, and without much curiosity, what unknown things they might be doing when they were not in here, or on the golf course, what dashing events and excitements filled their days. That was all a part of the idyll of the place, its space and air and wide sky.

I knew that some, in their other lives, were stock-brokers, whatever that was. I had no wish to find out. I was not anxious to know about any of these people, because I was obscurely aware that knowledge could only compromise the charming mystery of their lives, lives which were a part of houses I had never been into, seeing only their sea-bleached cotton curtains blowing in the sunshine.

The Spicers (he was 'in paper') had the grandest house on the sea-wall, but I had heard my father remarking that Glucksteen could have bought out the lot of them.

JOHN BAYLEY

Why Nancy Glucksteen's father, always chuckling and chatting away in the Mixed Room, should have wanted to do such a thing I had no idea; and Nancy herself, a year or so younger than me, gave no impression of affluence. She was a nice plump little girl to whom I felt rather attached, although I did not want anyone to be aware of it, least of all Nancy herself. We sometimes watched the tennis on the courts near the clubhouse, and once as we were walking home together she said how romantic everything looked in the twilight, rolling her little black eyes at me. I thought this a silly remark but was rather touched too: vanity suggested this might be Nancy's way of saying she was fond of me.

Apart from the general fact that she belonged to the world of Littlestone there was nothing romantic about Nancy for me. I reserved such feelings for older girls, like Patricia Terry. Moving as she did in a world of sports cars and young men who wore silk scarves, Patricia scarcely noticed me, and I much preferred things that way; but once she came up to me in the Mixed Room and said, 'You read such a lot, don't you? Shall we two start a society called "The Readers"?' I fervently assented to this proposition, not grasping that she was teasing me, though in quite a kind way. Sunburned and handsome, a good tennis-player, she must have been nearly ten years older than I was.

Nancy Glucksteen's parents were over by the bar, in loud and hearty conversation with Mr Oberlander – Herr O as he was known. It was a nickname he encouraged. He was famous for his putting, which he took very seriously. When he sank a long putt on the eighteenth green he

[100]

would perform a little dance of triumph, waving his club in the air and chanting,

> 'Said the old Obadiah to the young Obadiah
> I am dry, Obadiah, I am dry.
> Said the young Obadiah to the old Obadiah
> So am I, Obadiah, so am I.'

The Glucksteens lived in the next house to Herr O and obviously got on with him very well. This would have been in 1933 or '34. The Glucksteens were certainly Jewish: Herr O very much a self-declared German. How did they really get on, and what did they think of each other? The strange thing is that both these families, as I now feel looking back, were, at least temporarily, innocent. Perhaps unconsciously they regarded the Littlestone world as a holiday and a refuge, something quite separated from whatever was going on in politics and public affairs.

The other possibility is that Littlestone was not innocent at all, any more than anywhere else at the time, or at any other time; and that the usual dislikes, envies and resentments were festering below the surface; the usual amounts, too, of marital misery, jealousies, affairs and intrigues, money worries . . . No doubt. But I still feel I was not entirely naïve in taking the idyllic nature of that little society for granted. It still seems so, even after all the things that have happened since, to myself and to the rest of the world. I have no idea what became of Herr O – was he interned? Did he see the signs in time and go back to Germany? – or what happened to the Glucksteens.

They live in the past. Patricia Terry is vanishing up the New Romney road in a sports car. On the eighteenth green Herr O is for ever singing his little song; Nancy is rolling her little black eyes at me and saying the twilight was romantic . . .

7

In 1943 I was called up into the army, from which I didn't escape until 1947, two years after the war ended. I dreaded the army just as I had dreaded school, but to my amazement I found it quite different, and infinitely preferable. The sheer relief of this discovery made the experience itself seem almost delightful. Soldiers were not a bit like the schoolboys whom I had so much disliked. There was no team spirit, no rivalry or censoriousness, and very little attempt at organisation.

My fellow soldiers or recruits were big and clumsy, unworldly and uncouth, kindly and fearful. Unlike the correct public schoolboys I was accustomed to they made no attempt to hide their feelings, and their apprehension and misery at finding themselves away from home for the first time. They were helpless; they missed their mothers dreadfully: in the adjacent bunks of the crowded barrack-room I could hear some of them weeping in the night.

It was a most comforting sound. I wished I could console them. No stiff upper lips here: they were openly and pathetically grateful for my sympathy, or anyone else's. Sometimes two of them would huddle together, and hold one another, as I had seen women do on the wartime railway stations. All this was deeply reassuring. Previously I had led my own life, inside my own solitary concerns. Now, and for the first time, I felt wholly at home with other people. I felt I could do everything the army expected of me – which was not much as it seemed – and do it as well as or even better than the others.

I even did my best at 'Physical Training', and the savage corporal with a curiously fluty voice who swore at us as we tried to negotiate rope nets and wooden horses at least recognised how hard I was trying. At weapon-training I earned the commendation of the sergeant for remembering the names of the many parts of the Bren machine-gun. When he covered my hand with his big brown fist as he taught me to pull back the bolt of my rifle and take the first pressure, I felt absurdly gratified by his saying reminiscently that it reminded him of the hand of a girl he once knew.

Soldiers in my experience could say such things without sounding either soppy or as if they were making a sexual advance. In fact I neither learned nor saw anything of homosexuality in the army, although I knew all about it theoretically from school, where my instinct had in any case been to keep away from everyone. Now a physical contact like the sergeant's hand, or a fellow-recruit putting an arm round my neck, merely seemed pleasurable and humane. I relished the camaraderie which in a very few days began to grow up between us all in the barrack-room. No more books and private dreams: all such things now seemed equally and entirely out of place.

Great then was my dismay when I was told one

morning to report to the Orderly Room. Although I had been only two months in the army I was already quite familiar with its little ways, and this could only mean trouble in some form. Nor was I wrong. I received instructions to report to the OCTU (Officer Cadet Training Unit) at Aldershot. I was also given seven days' leave. My kindly comrades commiserated with me. They crowed a little too. 'Cor, you'll catch it now, Johnny. They'll turn you into a fucking officer.' The only thing they envied me was the week's leave, a pearl beyond price.

I was warmed by their sympathy, but their frank amusement very much depressed me. It was going to be all right for them. I wanted only to stay with them in the snug barrack-room, with the undemanding routines and the total absence of responsibilities. I already disliked the officer types: they seemed much the same as boys at school. Without knowing it I had discovered, as many middle-class boys had done at that time and in those circumstances, the romance of the proletariat. It features in the poetry of the period – Auden and Spender – and in the outlook of the intelligentsia. It comes in Orwell, most obviously in *1984*. Romance is the right word for it. The lower classes were wonderful. Exploited and downtrodden as they were they remained the salt of the earth, the whisper of love, the hope of the future. Their mysterious culture was to be admired and emulated. It all seems very old-fashioned today.

I went on leave in a rather low state. It seemed an anti-climax. I knew that being at home would seem empty and meaningless now, just as Littlestone itself had seemed long ago, back for the holidays for the first time from school.

And so it proved. At the beginning of the war we had been living in a small London flat, which was bombed during the blitz in 1940. Something else had to be found, and my parents had been offered a small house at Gerrards Cross, to rent for the duration. There I had soon become just as attached to the woods and wild places round about as I had been to the open skies and the sunlit links of Littlestone.

The woodlands near which we lived at Gerrards Cross are now bisected with the motorway and dotted all over with desirable residences. But during the war years all was peace and rural quiet and stagnation. Grass already sprouted through the newly madeup drives and roads; no hiker or tripper walked in the wild glades, full of golden beechleaf drifts and Rose Bay Willowherb. Rare White Admirals, one of the most beautiful and least gaudy of all butterflies, flitted ghostlike along the lush damp woodland rides. I had private holes and lairs among the Macrocarpa and Lawson's cypress where I lay reading, or attempting to write poems. Dreams of fair women, imagined but never encountered, mingled with the sights and smells of the woodland, and the resinous odour of the conifers on hot days.

This period too was now over and past. Home on leave I saw that all too well. In my last schooldays at Gerrards Cross I had been fond of Katherine Mansfield's Journal, and had marked the passage where she says, 'I shall not walk with bare feet in wet woods again.' She must have been just developing the tuberculosis which eventually killed her. Now I felt, or felt I felt, the same. For me too the woods were over, just as the dunes and links of Littlestone had been. I would have to stop going backwards instead of forwards. The future had come upon me, as the curse came upon the Lady of Shalott in Tennyson's poem.

But just for the moment I welcomed it. I did not in the least worry about the war, the army, all the unknown life that was to be. I recognised that I was in limbo, and the sooner I got back among my fellow-soldiers the better. I remember being surprised at the sheer unusualness, in me, of this state of mind.

But in 1943 everything seemed to be on the move. Even my parents appeared to have caught the prevailing mood and to be as preoccupied with getting on with their job, or the war, as everybody else was. My mother worked long hours in a soldiers' canteen; my father, having made desperate but unavailing attempts to get back into something military, had got himself temporarily into the aircraft business. My brothers were both in the army. I scarcely saw either of them during the war. One was to be captured by the Germans during the advance north of Rome; the other was seriously wounded in 1945 at the Rhine crossing.

Lying in bed with Iris beside me I think about those comparatively recent years, as they now seem to be. What was she doing then, in those years before I met her? She had been a grown-up person during the war, and I had scarcely been that. She had finished 'Greats' at Oxford – the demanding four-year course in classical literature, history and philosophy which only the best and most intellectual students could tackle – and she had at once been drafted for the duration into the Treasury, the top flight of the civil service. After working there a short time she became the acknowledged expert on one of the trickiest fiscal concepts which had arisen during the emergency period. This was 'National Promotion in Absentia', and it related to the complex problem of pay ratio. What might a functionary have been earning, what status in the hierarchy might he have achieved, had he not been called to the colours on the outbreak of war to serve his country in a more warlike capacity?

There is always something intriguing about the hypothetical. Imagining Iris at her desk in Whitehall (she showed me the window once, quite close to the Parliament buildings) I imagine too the life she was living there, and the far from notional steps and decisions she might have taken in her private life – happenings which would have ensured that I never met her. Her brilliant and creative mind, preoccupied for many hours a day with the niceties of bureaucratic business, contrived to function none the less in other fields, notably in a hunger for the kinship of her kind: people with whom she could argue about the arts and discuss literature, people with whom she could fall in love.

Wartime London was in many ways far more active intellectually and artistically – emotionally too no doubt – than it has ever been since. Those were the great days of magazines like *Horizon* and *Poetry London*, for whose cultural offerings there was an extraordinary appetite among both civilians and the armed forces. Cyril Connolly's highbrow *Horizon* would actually be passed from hand to hand in barracks and mess rooms, the troops appreciating its bland refusal to concern itself with any sort of wartime propaganda.

Iris met Cyril Connolly, Stephen Spender, and Arthur Koestler (whom she instantly disliked, a rare thing for her) and she became a friend of Tambimuttu, the charming and eccentric little Sri Lankan editor of *Poetry London*. Her more serious contacts dated back to her time in Oxford, where all the young men had adored her. She had probably been closest emotionally to Frank Thompson, the brilliant elder brother of our contemporary historian E.P. Thompson.

Frank had joined the special forces in 1944, fighting undercover in Greece and the Balkans. Captured by the Bulgarian army after a misdirected parachute drop he was shot along with the other partisans. Iris told me that she and he had not been in love exactly – they had been so full of their own work and their own play – but the waste of his death seemed an almost mortal blow to her own powers of living, and one from which they took many months to recover. Recover in a sense she did, to fall in love with other men, men as remarkable in their own way as the hero who had died in the Balkans. Destiny might, as I later felt, have promoted any one of them. But Iris remained like a star, shining and single in the middle of her constellations. And neither of us knew of the other's existence.

For me the army had become like a womb. Birth into a terrifying world of military realities could not be far away and yet gestation continued to prolong itself. For months

JOHN BAYLEY

I was sent here and there, on this 'course' or that; all designed, as it seemed, to further my military education; and yet there were no exams to pass, and no special penalties for poor performance. The army seemed to value good manners above dedication and high achievement. Once, after I had returned to the home counties from distant Catterick, where I had been instructed in the art of the Four Point Two Inch Mortar, the Adjutant of our unit sent for me. He was gazing thoughtfully at a sheet of paper. Standing to attention I saluted but he did not look up at me. It seemed to take him a very long time to read the page on the desk before him, and I wondered haplessly what horrors it could contain.

Had I done so badly that he was about to invite me to leave His Majesty's Service? Would I be sent down a coalmine instead, or on board a destroyer? The Adjutant, a gangling kindly man with weak eyes and an always immaculate tunic and Sam Browne belt, hardly knew how to put the worst into words.

Finally he looked up and said, 'It's an interesting report, Bayley. Very interesting. Does you credit on the whole. It seems you set a good example. Always tried to do your best. Various mishaps. It seems you had difficulty getting the hang of it. But you always managed to cheer them up. That's what it says.'

He looked puzzled for a moment, as if finding it hard to grasp how I might have accomplished this feat. Then his face broke into the kindest of smiles. 'So it all seems eminently satisfactory,' he said. 'Very good. Keep up the good work.' And he dismissed me with a courteous little gesture.

The irony of the 'report', good-humoured as it was, seemed to have been lost on the Adjutant's own impenetrable courtesy. In view of some of the things that had taken place while I had been put in charge of the Four Point Twos while on exercises, I felt greatly relieved. The instructor, a saturnine captain with three wound stripes on his arm, had shown no sign whatever at the time of being cheered up by whatever errors and miscalculations I had been responsible for. Indeed they had caused him at times to indulge in fits of hysterical rage, obscenities flowing freely from a mouth horribly deformed by the wound inflicted by a German 88 in North Africa.

But it seemed that he had not held these incidents against me. Perhaps they had indeed helped to cheer him up after the event, distracting the inner traumas from which he was all too evidently suffering? In any case when it came to writing that report he had behaved, as it now seemed, like a gentleman.

As a result I was put in charge of the Three Inch Mortar Platoon, smaller weapons than the big Four Point Twos and requiring less expertise in their operation. It was hinted that my custodianship might only be temporary, until a more suitable permanent appointment could be made. I did not mind that. As a Second Lieutenant, the most disposable and unconsidered rank in the army, I was accustomed to look no further than whatever stroke of fortune might befall. '*De minimis non curat exercitus*', to adapt the old legal proverb: for good or ill one was too low to be much bothered about.

More to the point perhaps, it was in expectation of a bloodbath, after the Second Front and the serious fighting should begin, that the army had created too many junior officers. The army was expecting something like the first day of the Somme, in 1916, and fortunately nothing quite so bad as that was to take place. Some of my contemporaries were promoted and sent overseas; some were wounded or killed; but a sizeable surplus, of which I continued to be one, remained.

Such calculations seemed far from anyone's mind at the time, and I looked forward to taking out the Three Inch Mortar Platoon on exercises, well away from the supervision of authority. Our tube-like weapons were carried in tracked vehicles, like a miniature open-decked tank, and in these we could roam the deserted wartime roads at will, seeking suitable sites to set up our apparatus and practise a leisurely shoot. Sometimes these were practice affairs – 'going through the motions' as it was known in the military vernacular. Sometimes our voyages took us to a regular firing range, where the crews would vie with each other to feed the mortar Moloch at top speed like jugglers, and see how many of its projectiles could be kept in the air at the same time.

At first I was secretly frightened of the creatures, and of my turn as a member of the crew who stood by the uptilted gaping muzzle and slid the finned bomb swiftly into it – the right way round of course. There had been accidents when some clumsy soldier had put the bomb in fuse-end downwards, and it had exploded at the bottom of the tube. It had also been known for the hand or hands of the crewman to be taken off by the emerging bomb, if he were not smart enough in removing them from the muzzle. It could even happen that an over-adroit and over-zealous handler might get another bomb down the spout before the previous one had time to emerge.

All these possibilities received a mention during our early training period, retailed in various styles of military humour. They were vividly present to my imagination when we first practised with live mortar bombs, but what was the use of worrying, as the troops used to sing in the first war. I soon got used to ladling the bombs down the spout with the same careless ease as the rest of the platoon. The big Four Point Two on which I started training was a more sober weapon, fired by a lanyard pulled well back from the mortar, and its rate of fire was nothing like so frenetic as its sprightly junior, whose bomb simply hit a spike at the bottom of the tube and was instantly ejected with an ear-splitting crack. I used to surreptitiously stuff my ears with bits of paper, concealing this timorous practice from the rest of the platoon with the straps of my steel helmet.

I had two particular friends and allies on these expedi- tions. One was Sergeant Eastwood, the oldest man in the platoon, who actually came from Eastwood, the midland town near Nottingham where D.H. Lawrence was born. Invalided home from active service in Italy he was strongly in favour of a quietistic approach to the routine of our daily training. In this I found him supportive, though he was an NCO of few words and his manner towards a very junior officer like myself carried a degree of patronage as well as a mild edge of contempt.

Though I did not make any such comparison at the time, Sergeant Eastwood was a bit like the Gerda of my childhood, those distant days at Littlestone-on-Sea. His surly silent company was distinctly soothing of an evening, when if we were out on an exercise we sometimes sat in a pub together, drinking weak wartime beer. I did not like beer, but I supposed it was the sort of thing one should drink. Once Sergeant Eastwood offered to stand me a whisky. He had become friendly with a landlord who kept a supply under the counter. Taking this hint I was prompt afterwards to ply him with spirits when we could get them, on the grounds that we had had a hard day. He preferred brandy to whisky, having acquired a taste for it overseas, and we discovered one pub which still possessed a good supply. For the first time I discovered the pleasures of becoming soberly drunk, and when we returned late in the evening to the barn where we slept on such outings the sergeant sometimes laid a guiding hand on my shoulder.

My other friend and companion on these excursions was our driver and mechanic, a lance-corporal always known to the platoon as Curly. In the army the nickname is usually given to soldiers with heads unusually flat and straight, or to elderly-looking storekeepers with hardly any hair at all. Curly was an exception. His curls were indeed spectacular: arranged in symmetrical waves, which sprang out intact and erect whenever he took off his military cap.

Naturally I never used his nickname, always referring to him correctly as Corporal Perivale. He himself came from that part of London; but strange as it now seems the remarkable coincidence that Sergeant Eastwood came from Eastwood and Corporal Perivale from Perivale never then occurred to me. Nor, I think, to any other member of the platoon. Part of the fatalism of the Forces is that oddities of all kinds were taken for granted, and accepted without comment or surprise.

Although an expert mechanic Curly had been a window-dresser at Selfridges in civilian life, and he was a great one for the girls. I had reason to know this because he once approached me confidentially and enquired whether there was any chance of our taking a 'recce' – reconnaissance – by ourselves. Did I perhaps wish to investigate a new and interesting training area while the rest of the platoon were on routine exercise? I was naturally curious about Curly's motives, but he said no more at the time and I did not enquire further. A few days later some occasion did arise when we could go off by ourselves and I remarked as much to Curly, who looked jubilant.

We set off, traversing Chiltern beech wood country with which we were both familiar, until he halted the mortar carrier on a village green where, as far as I could remember, I had not been before. But it seemed that Curly had. With a hurried word of apology he climbed out of the vehicle and disappeared through the back door of a sizeable house. Minutes passed. The sun was warm, the village green peaceful. Dozing contentedly, as one often did during the idle moments in the army, I waited for quite a long time.

At last I felt this had gone on long enough. Should I go and see what had happened to Curly? I felt it might be bad manners to do so. At that moment a lady carrying a shopping basket came out of the front door. She saw the carrier, with me sitting in it, and looked a little surprised. She was about to walk on to do her shopping or whatever it was, but then, seeming to change her mind, approached the carrier.

I sprang up, but the vehicle was not easily quitted for the purposes of an introduction. When I scrambled clear at last she looked amused. 'Would you like some tea?' she said. Women everywhere in those days were accustomed to giving tea to soldiers, who were known to have an insatiable thirst for it. My undignified exit from the carrier and the smile on her face made me wish to keep our acquaintance as short as possible, so I made some noise of polite deprecation, indicating that I did not want to interrupt her morning's shopping.

'Oh, that's all right,' she said. 'Done any time. Who are you? I didn't know we had any troops round here.'

She spoke rather as if with the royal 'We', and her blunt 'Who are you?' seemed less interested in me personally than in the nature of the military organisation I represented. Taking it in the latter sense I told her, but she seemed scarcely to hear. We were through the front door by this time and into a large room filled with books in shelves and on chairs and tables, and decorated in a dashingly flamboyant manner which in some way both excited and intimidated me. *Horizon, Penguin New Writing* and Walter de la Mare's new anthology *Love*, with its stylish but romantic cover, were strewn over a wide elegant marble table with a raised bronze edge.

This was clearly no ordinary country lady. Though I felt shyer with her every moment my excitement continued to rise as well. After so many months in the army the sight of books, and all the latest and most in vogue books, had an intoxicating effect on me.

'Do sit down,' she said, and I did so reluctantly, on an upright chair by the table. I would much rather have been allowed to wander round and have a look at everything. But good manners hardly permitted that.

No more was said about tea, and the silence grew rather awkward, though it did not seem to worry my hostess who continued to look at me in a quizzical way, almost, I thought, as if wondering what kind of use could be made of me. She was a big tall woman with fair hair and a strikingly large face and long neck. Much later I was to hear Lord David Cecil, my professor at Oxford, remark that she seemed to loom over you like a ship's figurehead. So indeed she did.

Feeling a bit confused I looked down at the table and saw some proof sheets corrected boldly in red. At the top of the page was a title 'Happy Holidays', and a name, 'Rosamond Lehmann'. I stared unbelievingly. Could this really be the woman whose novels I had read with such an intensity of pleasure, whose stories I had devoured in *Penguin New Writing* just before the army called me up? Surely there must be some mistake? This big, over-powering, and as I thought rather tiresomely upper-class woman could not be the unimaginably remote and sensitive and understanding person (rather like myself I had thought) who had written those novels and stories? I had yet to learn that writers when you meet them seldom seem in the least like their books.

Rosamond Lehmann, if indeed it was she, was looking at me now in an even more quizzical way, but with a complacent glance which somehow touched me. Probably my face had given me away. But how to make matters clear, in a mannerly and tactful fashion? She saved me the trouble. 'I see you know my writing,' she said, with a regal forward swoop of the head that brought her big features quite close to my face. She smelt strongly but most alluringly of some very grand scent or face-powder.

From then on it was easy. I chattered away about how much *Dusty Answer* and *The Weather in the Streets* had meant to me. For days they had bemused me into a thrilling grown-up world, but I did not use the word 'grown-up'. 'What do you think would have happened to them all,' I ventured, 'after the book was over?'

She looked kind and pitying for a moment, as if to a literary and worldly innocent. But she looked seriously gratified too. I was promising material, I would learn: and in the meantime I had paid her a compliment. 'Ah,' she said, adopting a slightly histrionic manner (many of her family were or had been on the stage) –

'What a dusty answer gets the soul
When hot for certainties in this our life . . .'

Some time later, after we had talked a good deal about hers and other books she started laughing. 'Here am I keeping you from your duties,' she said. I thought wistfully how proper it was that she seemed to have none of her own. I liked the idea of such a distinguished idleness in wartime.

'Let's go into the kitchen,' she said. 'My cook must

have some cake she could give you, and perhaps tea is on too.'

She led me across the passage and opened a door. There sat Curly with his arm, and indeed his leg too, around the cook, an attractive woman built on the same heroic scale as her mistress. They disentangled them-selves, looking pink and rather dishevelled, the cook especially so.

'Oh, never mind us,' said Rosamond Lehmann, shut-ting the door and leading me back into the drawing-room. She made no further reference to what we had seen, but took a book from amongst many of the same kind on a shelf and scribbled her name in large letters on the flyleaf. It was *The Weather in the Streets*, but I have a recollection that her latest book, *The Ballad and the Source*, was just about to come out.

She gave me the book with a smile, and then plucking it back demanded my name. My stammer overcame me and I could hardly get it out. 'John will do fine,' she said writing it. 'My brother's name too.' And she dismissed me with great ease, saying, 'Come again.'

I knew as I walked exultantly back to the carrier that I had been wiped instantly off her mind, but that was only proper and it did not depress my spirits in the least. More pleasing still was the earlier glance that seemed to want to make something out of me. I did not then interpret her interest as the one some writers can assume as painters do, summing up the human material in front of them in terms of composition.

I thought perhaps I might find myself figuring in one of her *New Writing* stories: perhaps a young officer, rather

sweet really, who appeared from nowhere one morning?
. . . Lost in the daydream I felt caught up into heaven,
like Jacob in the Bible.

Curly was sitting very upright in the driving-seat of the
carrier, with the air of a patient chauffeur. I climbed in
beside him and we started off without a word. With their
steel tracks and exposed Ford V8 engine, carriers made a
frightful din and were not suited for conversation. I sat
rapt in a dream, hugging my book to me and thinking of
writing; and the immense good fortune of having met a
great writer, one whom I so much admired.

I am not sure now that Rosamond Lehmann is a great
or even a very good writer, although she has a force and
a flavour of her own, and her earlier books survive pretty
well. Elizabeth Bowen, whom I knew later when she had
become a friend of Iris, used to say that Rosamond was
a loose cannon, always charging into other people's lives
and having her own life knocked about in consequence.
The poor woman was certainly knocked about, losing
the poet Cecil Day Lewis, the great love of her life, to
Jill Balcon the actress, who was later to become a friend
of ours; and her much loved young daughter to polio in
Singapore. That became the subject of a late novel, *The
Swan in the Evening*.

When I encountered her by chance on that village
green in the Chilterns she had, at least to my innocent
eye, an air of inviolability, as if none of the mean and
commonplace woes of life, with which I felt myself
already familiar, could come anywhere near her. Her
books of course show the opposite. There is a strong
odour of unhopefulness about them, more realistic and

chilling I now feel, than in, say, Hardy's novels. Other
odours too. Rachel, David Cecil's wife and daughter of
the literary critic Desmond McCarthy, used to say that
Rosamond's novels reminded her of a very grand Ladies'
Cloakroom. Scent and toilet-water and face-powder, and
under it all a hint of things not so pleasant.

After we had driven a few miles on our homeward
road Curly turned the roaring carrier off into the yard
of a transport café where we had often been accustomed
– sometimes just the pair of us, sometimes the whole
platoon – to refresh ourselves with 'tea and a wad' –
the soldiers' equivalent of the office coffee break. I had
supposed Curly to be sufficiently refreshed already, but
I suspected he wanted the chance of a little private chat
about what had just taken place.

I was determined to ask no questions myself. I was
more than happy with the book I had acquired, which I
brought in with me in case it should be removed from the
open carrier (books were surprisingly valuable objects at
all levels of wartime society), and also with my memory
of the meeting.

''Course I can see you read a lot, Sir,' Curly began in
a kindly way, eyeing the book in my hand, and as if
to demonstrate a preliminary magnanimity about such
habits, which he would soon have to be telling me, none
the less, could go on if unchecked to be the cause of
impotence or blindness.

I felt slightly nettled by Curly's line, since I felt he
had some explaining if not apologising to do himself,
having kept me waiting outside in the carrier while he
had caroused over limitless tea and cake in the kitchen,

astride the majestic cook. But since I had had my own windfall, in the shape of a meeting with the fabulous Rosamond Lehmann, it would only be fair to be magnanimous myself.

'Have you known her long?' I asked, wishing out of politeness to seem warm and interested in Curly's lovelife. I supposed it would follow what I took to be the normal if to me still inconceivable progress of amorous ritual: dalliance, engagement, followed after a short or a longer interval by marriage. Sentimentally I supposed they had been seeing each other at weekends in the teashops of Henley or Reading, and exchanging tender epistles. Curly would no doubt have sought to devise other ways of meeting his lady-love, and to use the carrier for this purpose must have seemed a heaven-sent opportunity.

I enjoyed imagining the strange but touching ways in which other people behaved, and was glad now to show fellow-feeling with what I decided must be Curly's programme.

A look of utter incredulity passed rapidly over Curly's mobile features, to be succeeded by a kindly smirk. It was plain that the full depth of my unworldliness, the product no doubt of books, and the result of reading them, had been revealed to him in a sudden flash.

'Herb in Signals told me there were a couple of nice bits of stuff over at that village place,' he explained. 'So I thought it might be worth our while, Sir, to have a bit of a recce.'

I tried not to appear as discomfited as I felt. For a moment I even wondered if Herb in Signals, that unknown philanthropist, might not have set the whole thing up. Two nice bits of stuff, each of ample size, domiciled together? What a treat for his friend Curly and Curly's officer, since they had the carrier at their disposal!

But the philanthropy of Herb in Signals could hardly have extended that far. With a rapid feat of adjustment which I still feel to be rather creditable, considering how innocent I was, I now managed to favour Curly with a slight leer of admiration and fellow-feeling. Should I pretend that some sort of amorous passage had indeed taken place in the drawing-room, while he and the cook were locked together in the kitchen?

But I realised at once that the new book lying on the table would in itself at once belie such a claim. As if to confirm my thought Curly picked it up a moment and gazed incuriously at the picture on the jacket. An upper-class-looking couple, drinks in their hands, were just emerging through French windows into a garden. Curly put the book down again.

'She's a smasher, Sir,' he said solemnly. 'A real smasher. But I wouldn't want to go again. Bit too demanding, if you see what I mean.'

Curly smiled reminiscently, clearly confident, none the less, that I wouldn't have the slightest hope of seeing what he meant. He stuffed a large piece of the 'wad' into his mouth, as if to restore his primal vigour, taxed by his recent encounter with the cook. On his feet he made a mildly histrionic gesture, indicating extremes of exhaustion. It was time to go.

*   *   *

That was the Golden Age of my army service. The war was raging; the Second Front had begun, but routine and training went on in the same old comfortable way, with plenty of cosy incidents and a few memorable ones, like the encounter with Rosamond Lehmann. Sometimes the Three Inch Mortar Platoon went on longer training forays, extending over a couple of days and nights, as on the early occasion when Sergeant Eastwood and I had found the pub which possessed a supply of brandy.

In my spare time, and for reasons which my powers of recall cannot now fathom, I had taken to learning the descant recorder, having managed to buy one at the Dolmetsch shop in London when I was on leave. I must have been fascinated by the pure reedy sounds, and by the revelation of simple musical notes, which I mastered from the children's handbook supplied. The names of the little airs – 'Greensleeves', 'Go to Joan Glover', 'Sellinger's Round' – seemed in themselves a pure element of escape. Escape into the past, to a happier world. 'Escapist' was a word of those days, used rather disapprovingly, but with a hint of yearning none the less.

I was shy of trying to play the thing in barracks, except when the two other officers who shared the room were absent. But on exercises I could remove myself to a little distance and laboriously pipe an air or two, in slow time and with frequent pauses. Once Sergeant Eastwood heard me at it, and listened for a moment or two as if in incredulous resignation. What would these so-called officers get up to next?

'I should swing it a bit, Sir, if I were you,' was his only

comment as he stumped off to attend to some needful military chore.

The most ambitious of these expeditions was also to be the last. Nemesis was lying in wait, as is usual during a Golden Age. We were to go down to a large training area near Minehead in Somerset, the haunt of serious armoured vehicles, Churchill and Cromwell tanks. They had presumably all vanished away in ships across the Channel to the Second Front, and we had the large wild area by Exmoor to ourselves.

I was impressed by the beauty of the countryside, but as often happened in the army it was not possible to do much more than feel tantalised by beautiful places – military training never seemed to take place in ugly ones – which there was no way of appreciating. I felt I *did* appreciate them, but only as if I were a quite different person, not the same me who had haunted the links and shore of Littlestone and the woods of Gerrards Cross. I might have said with Coleridge in his 'Dejection Ode', 'I see, not feel, how beautiful they are.' I had not read the poem then, but I knew that Coleridge had lived at Nether Stowey, and I was thrilled when our carriers went clanking through the village, and I saw a dovecot on a high wall which I thought looked very Coleridgean.

No time to stop of course, even if I could have thought of a reason for doing so. Besides I had other things to preoccupy me – real worries. They came from the very fact which had made the whole idea of the expedition so delightful. We were supposed officially to have gone by train, with the carriers transported on flat cars. The necessary Movement Order had been issued. Then at the

last moment Corporal Perivale observed insinuatingly
that it would be much more fun to drive. I think he
fancied the idea of rampaging with his beloved carriers
for hundreds of miles, instead of on the short routine
trips to which they were accustomed.

I too saw the powerful charm of the idea, and I
allowed myself to be tempted. Sergeant Eastwood, when
consulted, merely smiled his sardonic smile and gave no
opinion either way. If trouble came later he was not to
be part of it.

On my own dubious authority I cancelled the Movement Order, and when the day came we set out by road,
chattering like a bunch of schoolboys. The maximum
speed of a mortar carrier was under forty miles an hour,
and Curly Perivale saw to it that the four vehicles vied
with each other in a race along the almost empty wartime
roads. There was next to no civilian traffic; all we met
was an occasional convoy of army trucks. Road signs
had been removed since the invasion scare of 1940, and
my simple task was to read the map. Between doing that
I could stand up in the leading carrier, with the March
wind blowing me about, and feel like Alexander at the
head of his army.

Disaster struck somewhere near Shepton Mallet. The
carrier behind me lost speed, started smoking, and finally
came to a halt. We all stopped. Curly got to work and
looked grave. 'Big end, Sir,' he reported. I had no idea
what a big end was but I could see that it seriously
mattered. We left the vehicle in a farmyard and drove
on, crowded into the surviving three. Not many miles
later another gave out. I forget what was wrong this

time, but to my surprise and relief Curly now looked positively cheerful. He explained that we should return to the stricken carrier and cannibalise it. That would do the trick. Hours later he and his mate triumphantly reported success. We set off again, towing the casualty, at Sergeant Eastwood's suggestion. He said nothing more, but I think he had the canny idea that authority might be less displeased if we at least arrived with all our military gear, instead of abandoning some of it on the way.

Our convoy was now very slow, and night began to fall. I was becoming more and more conscious of the unwisdom of cancelling that Movement Order. But then we had a stroke of luck. We passed a large camp, full of American soldiers. On an impulse I stopped at the gate and asked the sentry if we could come in. With that American friendliness and casualness which seemed to us so delightful during the war he raised no objection. The irrepressible Curly admired his Winchester carbine, an exotic weapon quite unknown to the British Army, and the sentry obligingly let him examine it. The Commandant was obliging too when I explained our predicament and asked if we might spend the night with him. 'Sure, boys, sure. Make yourselves at home.' We did; feasting in the mess room on unheard-of quantities of ham and eggs, blueberry muffins, pecan pie . . . And we slept between sheets – a great luxury – in a vacant hut.

I was a little uncertain of our reception when we arrived at the Minehead camp next day, but the CO there seemed not to have heard of our change of plan and was sympathetic about the breakdown. We covered ourselves with glory too, as it happened, by our part in a set-piece infantry attack in which we were allotted the task of giving covering fire. Real fire. We plastered the hillside where the enemy was supposed to be with our mortar bombs, and after the exercise the plywood targets were brought in for inspection. They were gratifyingly riddled with shrapnel holes and I told the platoon I was proud of them. This was an error, to remember which makes me grow hot and cold with embarrassment to this day. Sergeant Eastwood looked disgusted, the rest of the platoon merely uncomfortable.

But all was forgotten and forgiven when we set out next day for an exercise on our own, crammed into the surviving carriers. We roamed over Exmoor and found an idyllic campsite by a moorland stream. Our only accident that day had been the refusal of one of the mortar bombs to go off when it landed. This was a rare eventuality and there was a drill for dealing with it. The officer in charge – it had to be the officer – approached the unexploded bomb with circumspection and laid beside it a fused cone of plastic explosive which smelled of marzipan and gave one a headache if handled too long. The fuse was then lit with a special match and the officer proceeded at a dignified pace under cover. I knew the drill though I had never had to perform the operation before. I set out across the heather with my apparatus, and happening to glance back became aware of Sergeant Eastwood behind me.

I stopped. This was most irregular. Only one person, and he an officer, was supposed to do the job. I pointed this out to the sergeant. He looked unconcerned but obstinate, and I had no choice but to let him follow me. The bomb was easily found – it had a scarlet band round its bulbous middle – and I knelt down to perform the task, very conscious of the watching sergeant. When the fuse was lit both of us walked 'without haste', as the drill prescribed, to a big boulder we must have marked independently, and got well behind it. The sergeant winked at me – the only comment he made throughout – and after the successful explosion we walked in silence back to the platoon.

The sergeant had rum with him, and he gave me a tot that evening as we lay on the green bank of the stream. The rest of the platoon was larking about by the water, some distance off. Presently the balmy evening silence, with a single curlew calling somewhere, was disturbed by a muffled explosion. Agreeably muzzy with rum I wondered without much concern whether one or more of the men had managed to blow themselves up. We lay smoking peacefully, and soon there was another explosion. This time I felt a shade alarmed and glanced over at the sergeant who merely winked at me, for the second time that day. Soon there were cries of enthusiasm from downstream and the soldiers came tumbling back to us, their hands full of things that glistened and wriggled.

Fried in our mess-tins and eaten with hunks of army bread and mugs of strong sweet tea those moorland trout were delicious. I felt a little upset about the fate of the trout, blasted unconscious in their beautiful native element by plastic explosive which I, as the officer, was alone allowed to handle, and of which I was supposed to be the careful custodian. Naturally I never enquired how

[129]

the soldiers had got hold of it. Sergeant Eastwood was obviously implicated in the conspiracy, if not its prime mover, his task to keep me happily occupied while the dirty work went on.

I ate the trout none the less. There were plenty to go round, since many in the platoon turned up their noses at the idea of eating fish, or at least fishes that had never been properly exposed for sale on a fishmonger's slab. Sport, rather than gastronomy, had been their motive. 'Some of the lads have got a proper headache this morning, Sir,' said Sergeant Eastwood next day with his sardonic grin. That came from too much handling of the plastic explosive.

The early March weather was unusually fine and warm, and we basked in it. But there was a day of reckoning still to come, for Curly and for Sergeant Eastwood as well as for me. The carriers' caterpillar tracks and sturdy bodies had got mired in the bogs of Exmoor; and on Sunday afternoon, with nothing much else to do, Curly must have decided to take them across the firm sand and shingle and into the sea, to give them a good wash. He was very proud of the carriers, and zealous about their smart appearance. All had gone well apparently until the drivers attempted to reverse them from the shallow water in which they and their steeds had, as it were, been paddling. Then it was found that the sand was not so firm after all: the carriers were immovable. With Herculean efforts the men managed to drag one out by brute force; the other two stayed stuck.

By this time I had got the news and was on the scene, but there was nothing to be done. The tide was coming in. With set pale face Curly went from one to the other of his stricken monsters, removing carburettors and other of the more delicate pieces of mechanism from their insides. Presently nothing was visible of the carriers above the waves but the tops of their steel sides.

A Court of Enquiry was held. I was myself of course responsible, but the Commandant knew quite well how things were when it came to the causes of such an accident. Both Curly and Sergeant Eastwood were put on a charge. I was reserved for higher judgement and sent back alone to our parent unit. The cancellation of the Movement Order, the breakdown of the carriers on the road, and their final immolation in salt water – a crane had had to be ordered to pull them out – all lay heavily against me.

The Adjutant was as courteous as ever, but I was posted overseas, to war-torn Holland on the borders of the *Reich*, with the next draft, about a fortnight later. This might have happened anyway in the course of routine, and no suggestion of punishment was hinted at. The army showed all its remarkable powers of tolerance, and toleration. I still marvel today at the way these seem to have been exercised during the war.

I never saw Curly and Sergeant Eastwood and the platoon again. I did not miss them or they, I'm sure, me. But in memory we seem to have had a jolly time together for a while, in the way that such things sometimes happened in the army, at least in my later – much later – recollection. That, for all of us, was perhaps something to be thankful for.

8

Memory has a much larger appetite for small things than for anything on a scale not easily managed. The last days of the war, the last days of German resistance in their own backyard, are for me now only a blur.

Perhaps because of what had taken place in the Three Inch Mortar Platoon when I was in charge I had no further acquaintance with these weapons but became a supplementary Infantry Platoon Commander, waiting for whatever officer was in charge of a platoon to become a casualty. When someone did I was posted to a front line company, and for the few remaining days the war continued I saw what the languid officer meant whose only comment on warfare is alleged to have been, 'My dear! – the noise, and the people.'

Noise and people are in any case not friendly to the habitat of the 'intellectual being', and the memories that wander through eternity in the early morning, as I lie waiting for another day of caring and looking-after to begin.

I know there is a law of the conservation of energy, although I'm not sure how to define it. There is certainly a law of the conservation of trouble, the troubles we must all undergo in this vale of tears. If some are taken away,

by God or the government or scientific discovery, we can
be sure not only that the ones which remain will seem
more burdensome than before but that quite new and
unexpected ones will appear. Cancer may be cured; we
may all live longer and healthier lives. But a new disease
will be discovered: we shall find fresh cause for boredom,
dissatisfaction and misery in the longer time we have to
experience them.

Fortunately there is also a law of the conservation of
pleasure. In bed in the morning, waiting for the day
to begin, I comfort myself with this knowledge. Thank
goodness for it. As troubles get worse, small satisfactions
increase, both in intensity and in expectation. I look forward with passion to the moment after I put Iris to bed.
I come down, pour myself a drink, and while enjoying
it read a page or two of a book, some old favourite that
is lying near the kitchen table. Nothing new – never a
newspaper or periodical – but nothing old and famous
either, and nothing demanding. Something I have read
many many times before. It might be a Barbara Pym or
a James Bond novel, or Anthony Powell's *A Dance to the
Music of Time*, or a travel book by Ian Fleming's brother
Peter, or a history of the Hundred Years War, or Alan
Clark's *Barbarossa*. All these lie about within easy reach.

But Belial's method is best of all. Just letting the
thoughts wander. I should never have supposed before
that there could be so much positive pleasure in remembering things.

I cling to this pleasure grimly, as if I were holding on to
the side of a lifeboat. The pleasure boat. But remembering

is one thing – an innocent involuntary thing like Shelley's Spirit of Delight. Writing it down is another. There creeps into recollection the complacency which is also a part of memory. I am pleased with myself not only for remembering but for having recorded it in the mind with such precision. Most memoirs and autobiography have a 'clever little me' feel about them somewhere.

Thank goodness too that the summer is over – the hateful end of summer, which I dislike more and more the older I grow. A wonderful autumn has come at last, much more hopeful and reassuring than the spring. Down the road a tall Ginkgo tree, it must be the tallest in North Oxford, has turned pure Chinese yellow. The English beeches more bronze every day; chestnuts shedding leaves in all shades of pink and gold.

Our daily walks round the block are a real pleasure now. I would rather keep quiet about the trees, and enjoy them more that way, but I must try to enjoy them with Iris, and I keep pointing them out to her, not knowing it is the last time she will see the tints of autumn. She doesn't seem to respond. Does Alzheimer's take away the faculty of visual enjoyment, as well as of sense and coherence in the brain? I have a horrid feeling that I enjoy such things more and more now, because Iris does not, cannot, do so herself. It is not as if I was enjoying them for her, or trying to share my pleasure. More as if her inner desolation had stimulated my own receptivity, my own private powers of response.

It's depressing to see all this biologically. *The Woodlanders* again: Hardy's vision of the beautiful trees battening on one another, helpless not to profit from their neighbours' wounds and death. If the tree close beside me dies I have that much more light and air.

If I do it properly, with the proper degree of routine, Iris does at least still enjoy her supper. Lunch not. Perhaps there is invisible fellow-feeling between us there? One has to eat something about then, but one cannot be bothered with it. It is just a stage in the process of getting through the day. But supper is another matter – the day's crown and consolation.

Iris likes me to feed her then. I stand beside her like a serving-man in the Middle Ages and put each spoonful in her mouth – baked beans, tomato, bottled mayonnaise, a bit of Skipper's sardine. Then ice-cream and banana. Iris makes furry happy noises through all this. I feel happy too – my own drink and book and supper are not far away – and I can feel happy with her. No separation now, as when out on the walk, watching the trees. Now I can feel that Iris is aware of my happiness with her, perhaps she can even feel pleased that I am looking forward to my own solitary evening to come.

After the war in Europe was over we had all dreaded being sent off to the Far East, to fight the Japanese. But then that war was over too, and so I remained in Germany with the occupying forces. Demobilisation was not yet in sight – the earliest to be called up were the first to be let out – but there was not much now for the troops to do. With no looming conflict in prospect training tended to languish.

I was eventually found a 'job' in T force – army abbreviation for Target Force – who were supposed to be removing useful bits and pieces from German factories. This was for the benefit of equivalent English firms who might wish to profit from examples of Teutonic expertise. In practice, as we heard later, the bits and pieces did not fit in England, or were worn out, or already obsolete. Our cunning opponents had seen to that, and in due course their own factories started up again with all the benefits of modernisation, and brand new equipment paid for at least partly by the British taxpayer.

Our good-natured commander, a silent smiling brigadier who liked his gin, had liberated one of the Volkswagen factories at the end of the war, so the unit had a good number of early Beetle models, which the more enterprising officers among us delighted to drive. They required a lot of gear-changing and double-declutching, like a vintage racing car, but they were exhilarating to travel in and had a marvellous heating system, well-suited to the German winter and a joy after the draughty trucks. I never aspired to drive a Beetle – I was too junior anyway – but I enjoyed riding in one with the Brigadier or the dashing captain who was his assistant, and listening to their tales of being put in charge of the moribund VW factory. Higher authority had offered it lock stock and barrel to Morris Motors, but Lord Nuffield swore he wouldn't touch a Beetle with a bargepole – he was in the business of building respectable motor cars.

I was thought for some reason to know German, which was why I got the job. I had little to do, but I learned German feverishly in order to make some pretence of doing it. When a blueprint or a piece of machinery had been commandecred, my task was to pay a visit to the factory and make sure they were delivering the goods as bespoke. In practice these visits were fairly infrequent, and I also had the services of a German interpreter, but it had been decreed that an authentic British officer was required to make sure that nothing underhand went on between this interpreter and the factory officials whom we met. It was not clear how I was to ensure that there was none of such potential monkey-business, but at least I constituted a token presence, a warning against any attempt at cheating.

Herr Braatz, our mild-mannered interpreter, had lost an eye on the Eastern Front when attempting to clear a Russian minefield. His eye-socket wept copiously as if for Germany's sins, which of course we never spoke of. We sat companionably beside the driver in the front of the icy truck, and conversed as we could about education and children and moral welfare, subjects of exquisite boredom when expounded in Herr Braatz's pedantic English; but I found his company soothing and congenial none the less.

In spite of the easy work and driving about with Herr Braatz there were days when I felt quite homesick for my comrades of the old Three Inch Mortar Platoon, and I missed Curly invariably remarking 'end of another perfect day', as we drove back past the barrack square in the evenings.

Such nostalgia was dissipated one morning when I was sitting in the office surreptitiously trying to read Goethe's novel about the Sorrows of Young Werther while pretending to be engaged in unit correspondence. A young woman was shown in. She was plump and rosy,

1. The young Iris; not long after we got married and looking "determined to make my mark", as she once said to her oldest friend Philippa Foot (photograph by Ida Kar).

2. Iris looking mischievous in 1990 (© Miriam Berkley).

3. Norah Smallwood in her office at Chatto & Windus (Hulton Getty Collection).

4. Aldous Huxley in California wearing what looks like a snakeskin tie. (Hulton Getty Collection).

5. The great Dr Canetti, one of Iris's earlier loves who I once thought of as the godmonster of Hampstead. This must have been taken when he was nearly 80, and living in Zurich, rarely visiting London. (Hulton Getty Collection).

6. Walking in the University Parks (© Miriam Berkley).

Family group snapped by David Bayley's wife Agnes. Three Bayleys (from right, David, Michael and John, Iris and our oldest family friend Gloria Richardson). From about 1985 we always had a week's summer holiday together, taking a "holiday home" somewhere in Wales or the West Country.

8. The desk where Iris wrote her last three novels, upstairs at Charlbury Road. I gave her the sewing box when we were married. She had asked me to buy her one and she was fond of it, we had jokes about it. But I don't think it was much used.

9. Cascob in Wales. John with Iris's biographer, Peter Conradi, Iris with Cloudy, the blue-eyed Welsh sheep dog who became the magic dog Anax in the last but one novel, *The Green Knight*.

10. In the kitchen, late 1998.

11. Moira (Second-in-command), Tricia (Head of House), Pat and Maureen. The wonderful staff at Vale House Alzheimer's Home, where Iris was radiantly happy in the last days (© Rob Judges).

very German in appearance but in an artless way, as if she were an English schoolgirl pretending to look like a German. She wore short white socks and a black skirt. It was part of the uniform, as I subsequently discovered, of the *Bund deutscher Mädchen*, female component of the Hitler Youth.

Addressing me respectfully in halting English she said she had been sent from the Autobahn office, where she worked as secretary. They hoped we would excuse the road repairs and alterations that were going on as a result of the wartime bombing. They trusted we would not be unduly inconvenienced? It was typical of the Germans to gently rub in the fact that we had been bombing them, while naturally saying nothing about what they had done to other people.

I made some suitable reply, speaking in my new German. It was the conceit of showing that I could do it, and the girl switched to her own language with an air of submission. For my benefit she spoke slowly and carefully, as if she were still speaking English. When I made a joke of sorts she laughed conscientiously.

I visited Hannelore very discreetly. We were not supposed to fraternise with the Germans. I always took a tin of corned beef or a packet of cigarettes. In practice the non-fraternising regulation was not taken very seriously, although it was applied more strictly in the case of officers than men, and if my visits became known I was well aware that the army would once more show its powers of toleration by removing me without comment to a worse job, probably supernumerary platoon commander in some training unit.

So I was careful. And the cigarettes and the bully beef always ensured my welcome. The mark had no value. Everything was done by barter. Ten cigarettes were like the single dollars in Russia which became the accepted currency after the collapse of the Soviet empire. I bought what seemed a good Adler typewriter from a senior colleague of Hannelore for twenty Player's. The man was delighted and Hannelore was happy to arrange the deal. She wanted perhaps to pay me back for the good things I had lavished on herself and her family: the Autobahn official did not know that they got much more from me *gratis* every week than I had given him for his typewriter.

But he had the last laugh. I had dreamed of learning to type and becoming a writer later on in Civvy Street. I did learn to type, after a fashion, but the Adler turned out to be rather like those bits and pieces we were removing from the German factories. It held together more or less until I returned to England, and then it broke down. There was something radically wrong with it; and no spare parts were available at home even if they had been in Germany.

My relations with Hannelore were not what might have been expected, or what I thought I would have liked them to be. I thought naturally, as any romantic twenty-year-old might, that I wanted her as a mistress. Whether I really did I now rather doubt. If she had done all the work, as it were, then I suppose I would have had no choice, but she had no idea, apparently, that the idea might be in my mind. It was certainly not in hers. No doubt she was a genuinely virtuous girl; in any case she took our relations for granted just as they were: a jolly friendship sprung up between me and her family.

That was really what suited me too. It would be a good idea to improve my German in her company and Hannelore loved to talk, to chatter away endlessly in her own language about anything and everything. We kissed a good deal – Hannelore received and returned them like someone playing ping-pong – but we never got warmed up. One clear sparkling night when we had gone out to admire the stars after drinking some home-brewed alcohol of her father's, I put my hands under her skirt as we embraced and attempted something more robust in the way of a clinch. She pushed my hands away, wriggling and giggling, and when we went in – her parents had gone to bed – she apologised for her brusque behaviour and said it was better for girls to keep such goings-on until after they got married.

She sounded quite confident about this, but the mention of marriage alarmed me. Could that be what she was thinking of? She looked at me in an embarrassingly unfamiliar and even loving way as she said it. When I kissed her and said I understood she seized me impulsively in her arms. Her breath smelt of the strong sickly homebrew, and her features resembled what the young German in the ballad calls a *Bild von Milch und Blut*. Hannelore really did look then as if her plump engaging face had been made of blood and milk. Picturesque in a way – no doubt Goethe would have enjoyed the effect – but somehow at that moment too biological. It would have been like making love to a young heifer.

My ardour was the more easily quenched because

Hannelore, disentangling herself from me, began to talk with enthusiasm about the summer holiday she was hoping to have on the North Sea island of Nordeney. Wouldn't it be *wunderschön* if I could meet her there? I said it would be, but the idea did not greatly appeal. For one thing it would be taking fraternisation a trifle too far; for another, there was no indication that Hannelore proposed to share a room and bed with me: indeed it seemed likely that such an idea had not even occurred to her. Such things were kept for after marriage, even when on a holiday on Nordeney.

In any case my demob papers came through a little earlier than expected. But as we said goodbye, after a last lavish presentation to her family of cigarettes and chocolate, the idea of Nordeney and our possible reunion still lingered. I would come to her there from England? I didn't of course; but we corresponded now and again over the next couple of years. My own affairs kept me from having any curiosity about hers, but it seemed she just went on living with her parents and working in the Autobahn office.

Six years later on, it must have been in 1953, my brother Michael, now a Lieutenant-Colonel, was stationed in Germany, somewhere near Düsseldorf. This was quite close to Kamen, the small town where I had been stationed and where Hannelore lived. On the impulse I asked if I might pay him a visit. He was acquiescent if not particularly enthusiastic. But as it happened he would be away on an exercise for a month or so, and if I liked I might borrow his car.

After a tedious train and boat journey from England I picked it up at the barracks. A fatherly mechanic in uniform handed it over, and told me to watch out for the overdrive. The car was a lordly creature, an open Mercedes of pre-war vintage. I drove it with caution, not using the perilous overdrive, and was soon in an area which I recognised. I had written to Hannelore, who had replied with great vigour and excitement. And so my brother was now *Berufsoldat*, an *Oberst*, and he was nearby in Germany! Could I not bring him with me for a visit? I had just time to reply that he was away at the moment – well away I hoped – but that I had borrowed his car, and would appear on Sunday morning. The times had worked out quite conveniently.

Hannelore's excitement about my brother was rather damping to the spirits, but while driving along I was able none the less to indulge a daydream. I had the romantic car – why shouldn't we drive down the Isar, or the Moselle valley, stop at a friendly *Gasthaus*, have a two- or three-day romance? It was a nice idea, even though I was well aware that daydreams seldom or never materialised, not at least in the form in which one has indulged them. Still, Hannelore's ideas might have changed a bit in the last five years?

The dilapidated house on Jahnstrasse looked just the same, though all around the *Wirtschaftswunder* was performing its miracle of reconstruction, and spreading abroad a new post-war German prosperity. Hannelore was out at church when I arrived, but her mother was there to greet me.

Frau Jenker was an admirable woman, as was her

husband, the gentle creature who sold beer at the local *Stube*. Frau Jenker seemed excited about something other than my arrival, although she was obviously pleased to see me, and proud of the Mercedes outside the door, shedding lustre and prestige on the house.

In the early days of our acquaintance she had confided to me that in the first alarming weeks of the British Army's occupation she had seriously considered arranging for Hannelore to be temporarily walled up – '*aufgemauert*' – to protect her from the brutal and licentious soldiery. In the Russian zone this simple expedient would hardly have sufficed. Even after the end of hostilities the Russians were in the habit of firing their sub-machine-guns into the walls of a house, to flush out any girls they suspected might be lurking there.

I remembered too that I had seen a girl raped by a Russian soldier when I had been sent to Berlin on T force business; and that was three or four months after the end of the war. We had permission from the Russian *Kommandatura* to enter their zone to retrieve some escaped scientist's furniture. Perhaps it was not furniture only – I never found out about that – but negotiations with the Russian authorities, in which I had had no part, had been protracted though apparently quite cordial.

Gazing now into Frau Jenker's ruddy and seemingly guileless countenance I remembered watching in surreptitious fascination as the soldier had worked on the girl in a sort of slow motion, like a spider giving its quietus to a fly. Like the fly the girl had seemed in some sense resigned to the soldier's methodical activities. It was impossible to tell how far, if at all, she was willing. Perhaps it had been a purely commercial transaction? I had, after all, brought those cigarettes and tins of corned beef to the Jenker household.

The corned beef and cigarettes must originally have made a difference, but this sterling woman had natural good manners and a kind heart. She had always seemed to take for granted my relations with her daughter, an only child with whom she was on close terms. No doubt she had sized me up effectively, and yet she seemed fond of me in an artless way, this foreign young thing in uniform – officer's uniform, could it be possible? – who had appeared laden with gifts in that grim period after the war, and who had now suddenly reappeared, driving a grand Mercedes car.

In her old innocently inquisitive way she fingered my grey flannel trousers and worn tweed jacket, clearly finding these garments something of a comedown after my military gear. And so my brother was now *Oberst*? A fine man he must be she was certain! – they would love so much to meet him.

At that moment Hannelore arrived, and her mother glowed at her while pointing me out. With her rosy cheeks shining like freshly scrubbed apples Hannelore looked just the same, except that she now seemed mildly embarrassed about something – perhaps the same thing – quite apart from my arrival – which her mother had seemed excited about?

I could not make out what this was, and the two women did not enlighten me. We had a lavish snack of hardboiled eggs and pickled gherkins, together with every sort of salami and German sausage. A spread which was startlingly different from the post-war years, though I forbore to comment on the change.

Frau Jenker seemed the one who was to reveal whatever was in the air. But she didn't – she started to wonder at the Mercedes instead, and then remarked how *wunderschön* it would be if she and Hannelore could have a ride in it. Of course I said yes, they must, how splendid! '*Ach Mutti*,' protested Hannelore, looking embarrassed again, but her mother overruled her, and in a few minutes I found myself back in the Mercedes, with Frau Jenker beside me and her daughter behind.

This was not at all how I had imagined things going, but there was nothing to be done about it. I felt I was the victim of some sort of conspiracy, hatched at short notice by Frau Jenker. What could they have in mind for me, beyond free transport for a shopping expedition? Was I to be married on the spot to Hannelore?

It was suddenly alarming to be in the power of these two unknown women, as they now seemed to me, and I began to regret my impulse to return to Germany and seek out Hannelore again.

The little industrial towns of the Ruhr are all close together, like the pottery towns of Staffordshire, and presently we were in the streets of one not far from Kamen, which I remembered driving through in army days. I was bidden to stop by a house very like the one in Jahnstrasse. Hannelore and her mother disappeared inside. I remained sitting in the car under the curious gaze of one or two local residents. It was a sunny autumn day, and I wondered what Michael, the *Oberst*, was doing on his army manoeuvres. Could it be Michael himself who these two women were now after? In this new Germany there seemed to be all sorts of new and sinister developments and spells. It was the same, and yet wholly different; and I began to feel nostalgic for the abject country in which T Force had cruised around with casual lordliness.

The door of the house burst open and its denizens came rushing out in a babel of chatter, Hannelore and her mother in the midst of them. They surrounded the car like a mob who might drag me out of it and string me up to the nearest lamp-post, although their shining faces were all wreathed in smiles. One of them was a tall young man with a mop of dark hair.

I now realised, with mixed feelings, that no one was paying any attention to me at all. This young man was the focus of interest. Amidst the babel of speech my understanding of the language seemed to have totally deserted me, but at last I made out that here was Hannelore's fiancé, and that he was just returned from Russia, where he had been a prisoner of war for nearly ten years. Neither Hannelore nor her parents had ever said a word about him. She had merely been waiting for him to reappear.

It is all hard to imagine in an age when counselling is offered for every minor misfortune. But after the war the Germans wanted to forget, or at least they didn't want to talk about what they might otherwise remember. It was guilt no doubt; but it was also a passionate wish to get away into the future, their own future – somehow, anyhow – and to forget the past.

Hannelore's young man – they turned out to have been

engaged since 1942, when he joined the army – had simply got left behind in the dark past which everyone wanted to forget. Including Hannelore herself? Evidently not. She had not forgotten, but what would she have done if I had said I wanted to marry her? In the old days in Germany?

I had no idea what her present feelings were, and had no way of finding out. Perhaps she hadn't any? It seemed such a long time since we had met on the sofa together exchanging juvenile kisses while she chattered, as it seemed, about everything under the sun. We had shared a sort of intimacy in those days, of which at the time I had been hardly conscious; but the memory of it, overcoming me in these new circumstances, made me suddenly and passionately desire her. I longed to kiss her red mouth, to force kisses on it, as I had never done before. And now I was a few days too late.

She was going to marry this young man who had come back from the dead. For they had never heard whether he was dead or whether he might be still alive, somewhere in Siberia. It was known that many thousands of German prisoners were still held in the labour camps.

There were a few moments during the next two days when I made some attempt to ask him about it all. His frank gaze – he had very blue eyes, like Hitler's, under his dark hair – never once met mine. He said nothing; he seemed to know nothing about himself, and what he had undergone. I quickly gave up, feeling guilty myself of some serious indecency; and somehow I felt quite sure that neither his own relatives nor Hannelore and her parents would ever ask him anything, or tell him anything either.

Some of us had known about the concentration camps, and met fellow-soldiers who had liberated them, but we had no real news of the Holocaust itself. The average German knew something; but said nothing. They could not have avoided seeing the packed freight cars which left departure platforms at the main stations, Cologne and Hamburg, Dortmund and Düsseldorf. They did not claim not to know where those freight cars had been bound. They said nothing about it. Like the war itself it was all over and done with, and not to be mentioned again. Least of all to the recent enemies who were now their allies and friends . . .

I found I had conjured myself back into a new country, in which the past had been told not to exist. The German capacity to pass an Act of Oblivion on themselves seemed at that time total and complete.

Hannelore was now as animated as the others. She drank quantities of beer when we all had a meal at the *Gasthaus* together, and made me eat the yolks of several fried eggs, which she neatly extracted from the white part and offered me on the point of a knife. She said in that way one got the maximum benefit from them. I felt she was offering me some sort of compensation for what might have been. Her fiancé she paid hardly any attention to.

Nor did he to her. Feeling in my turn that I must give him some compensation I asked if he would like to drive the Mercedes. It was an absurdly rash thing to do, because I had no idea what the insurance arrangements were, or even if he could drive properly – possibly he hadn't seen a car for ten years. But none of that seemed to matter: his sudden excitement and gratitude at the offer were quite intoxicating. It had been the right thing to do.

He drove us to the *Gasthaus*, he drove us home to Jahnstrasse, dropping various relatives on the way; and then, without being invited, he seemed to think it only natural that he should take the Mercedes back to his own home town.

Without kissing him goodnight Hannelore bade him be punctual in the morning as she wished to go shopping with the car. We drank some more of her father's beer and Hannelore announced that she would take me to the hotel where she had arranged for me to stay. It was a short walk and when we arrived she gave me the intimate kiss her fiancé didn't appear to have had. By that time I was much too tired and bemused to feel anything but desire for bed.

As I entered the hotel I suddenly realised that here was the very same T Force HQ I had once worked in. It must have been bought, rebuilt and done up after the army had left, five years before.

The Mercedes reappeared in the morning, but the fiancé couldn't stay – he was just beginning his new job in the municipal Welfare Office – so I was required to take Hannelore and her mother to Dortmund, for a day's shopping. For them it was a *herrliche Gelegenheit* – heaven-sent opportunity. Hannelore's trousseau was in question, and her wedding-dress and one or two other things, and 'Der John' was so helpful and so kind. At least the Mercedes had a big boot, so I didn't have to wait in it to guard the parcels.

I had intended to stay in Germany a week or ten days, but now I decided that, come what might, I would go home tomorrow. I would arrange to have had an urgent phone call from my brother, who had suddenly found he needed the car. Magic evenings of old, under the lamplight at Jahnstrasse, with Hannelore's huge and shabby old teddybear sitting beside us on the sofa, seemed wholly irrecoverable.

During that time there had been a few subdued lamentations from Hannelore's parents about the terrible scarcity of everything since the end of the war. Now there was brassy abundance everywhere, and loud confident German voices. Even the interior of Jahnstrasse had been redecorated with furry wallpaper in a virulent shade of green.

All of them, including the fiancé, were full of dismay when I said I must go. They urged me please to reconsider, to ring my brother and say it was not convenient, to drive at the weekend with the fiancé and fetch him – the *Oberst* – back among them. I almost feared they might detain me by force. And Hannelore, as I could see with a real pang, was deeply upset and disappointed. I had had my own daydream about what we would do together; but she, and her mother, had been going to make a proper use of me, and I honestly think that they expected I would enjoy it as much as they had been proposing to do.

And so I fled, without shame or dignity, to catch the midnight train from Düsseldorf. After returning the car to the barracks I passed the time at a cinema near the railway station which was showing Clouzeau's masterpiece, *The Wages of Fear*, dubbed into German. Like everyone else I was transfixed by the film, and its title seemed curiously appropriate. Then I sat musing in the quiet station over a glass of Dortmunder beer.

I wondered what Hannelore really felt about this young man who had come back to her. She seemed to take him so wholly for granted. And yet she had not seen him for ten years – he must be a complete stranger to her – while it was only five years since she had seen me.

In spite of everything I had felt that I knew her, and that she knew me. Perhaps that had caused the look of bewilderment – or was it disappointment? – that had sometimes appeared on her rosy face?

I wrote to her of course, with an apology, but I don't think I ever had a reply. And I never saw her again.

PART II

DESIRE

9

The speaker in T.S. Eliot's *The Waste Land* tells us that 'April is the cruellest month . . . mixing memory and desire.' For me those two come separately; and they come most often not in the springtime but in the autumn.

No time for them in the autumn of 1947 – I was young, and it is a long time ago. No time then to reflect on what was past or passing; to look back on the army and Germany and Hannelore.

Desire had hardly played a part in our original Hansel-and-Gretel relationship, and I had no difficulty in putting her out of my mind. I had a shot at desiring her in the abstract when the chance came to go back to Germany; and when I saw her in the flesh, and her fiancé too, I indeed longed, however briefly, to love and embrace her. But she had disappeared into marriage, and I felt no urge to see her again or to revisit the new Germany.

After leaving school in the autumn of 1943 I had gone up to Oxford to try for a scholarship. I was feeling doomed and fatalistic. My call-up summons had come: I had to join the army the day after the exam finished. History was supposed to be my best subject, although I was really only interested in its more picturesque aspects, such as the campaigns of Hannibal or the Duke of Marlborough.

We sat in the hall of one of the oldest colleges – University – and as we toiled away with ink and paper – there were no ballpoints in those days – a form was sent round on which we were required to enter the name of the college at which we would wish to become a scholar, in the event of winning an award. The choice was between four or five, one of which was New College. In the state of mind I was I gave the matter little thought, but it did occur to me that a new college might be easier to get into than an obviously ancient and august one such as University. Each of the four or five was offering a History Award, so I wrote down New College.

It was to prove a fateful choice. In retrospect it seems bizarre that we were all so clueless, and the arrangements so casual, but in the middle of the war Oxford was almost a ghost town, with most of the younger dons away fighting, or working at the great code-breaking centre at Bletchley. There was no one to tell us anything, except for the few broken-down old dons who were supposed to be supervising the exam. I had a perfunctory interview at New College, which I was surprised to find looked much the same age as the one in which I had written my papers.

But by then I had lost all interest in such matters. I could think of nothing but the awful prospect that would be facing me next day.

Possibly that is the right frame of mind in which to do an exam, as I got the award. The telegram announcing my success meant very little, for I was in such a state of bewildered happiness at finding the army so pleasant to be in that I could give no attention to anything else.

And at that moment Iris, whom I have never met or heard of, is giving her whole mental attention inside the Treasury to 'Notional Promotion in Absentia', while falling in love with numerous persons outside it.

Trains of random little memories trail along behind us on our morning walk. One of them amuses me, so that I stop, and try to remind Iris of it. It was in some book about the navy – Marryat? Forester? Patrick O'Brian? The Captain knocks his ship's biscuit on the table during a dinner party, and two weevils emerge. One is a fine plump tough-looking creature, the other wizened and diminutive. 'Which of the two would you rather have, Mr Smith?' enquires the Captain jovially of a shrinking junior midshipman. After a painful pause, 'Why, I suppose the bigger one, Sir.' 'Wrong, Mr Smith, wrong. In the navy you must always choose the lesser of two weevils.' Hearty laughter round the Captain's table.

Iris seems to take it in, but the weevils are obviously too much for her. I move quickly to something else that the weevils have suggested. The 'woolly-headed bastard'. One of her publishers, who had been in the navy, used to tell us about it. A rammer with a lambswool head for cleaning a five-nine, or a six-inch gun.

Iris still seems fully in tune with the woolly-headed bastard, which we often used to laugh at in former days, and it makes her laugh again. We go round the last corner of the block arm in arm, quite animated.

Carers, as I discovered, soon become experts at reading the physical symptoms and choosing a remedy from among the sedatives prescribed. When Iris has a wandering fit at two in the morning Promazine syrup seems the best bet. Pleasant to take and quite easy to get a spoonful down. As indispensable as that old woolly-headed bastard.

'Caring'. The inescapable word today. A postcard this morning from an old army friend whose second wife, much younger than he, developed Alzheimer's. I think he cheers himself up **by** sending these little offerings. When I knew him he was a spruce and stylish young man. Elderly and retired now he looks after his wife with great devotion.

'We are accompanied into the millennium', said the card, 'not by the Four Horsemen of the Apocalypse, but by the four Cavaliers in White Coats. *Compassion, Caring, Counselling, Compensation*'.

Iris is usually still asleep when I come up to bed after a TV thriller. I crawl in carefully without turning on the light. Last night there were soft stirrings as in a nestful of birds, and soft cheeping sounds. Opening an eye I saw a shape briefly silhouetted in the faint light from the fifteen-watt bulb in the passage.

Then sounds from below, muffled at first. Iris would be heaping up piles of clothes, or rearranging the cairns of books, stones, cups and shoes that have been assembled on the floor. Sometimes there is the sharp noise of something breaking.

I continue feeling wakeful and preoccupied, as I know

Iris does. In this state it is easy to become at one with Dr A's patients. Neither of us now will sleep till morning, and it is no use at the moment giving her a dose of the Promazine. I must gauge the right time for that – about five a.m. probably, when simple tiredness will assert itself, but not enough to calm her down without some chemical help. If I gave it to her now I know from experience that it would be useless. Mania would win.

In spite of the prospect of no sleep I feel calm myself, and professional, morale high. Gone (I hope) are the amateur days of my own tantrums, miseries and irritations, which Iris used to cope with by a kind of matrimonial reflex, a private version of the social one which can still on occasions stand her in good stead.

Undoubtedly one of the compensations, as the Alzheimer's gets worse, is the way in which the carer finds himself becoming two people: one closely identified with the sufferer and her symptoms, as I was with Iris's downstairs: the other in a state of almost enjoyable detachment, much aware of any treat he can save for himself.

Calmness and confidence are what doctors must enjoy: not only displaying them but feeling them too. Their own well-pleased and well-practised resources of calmness and confidence, whose detachment keeps the doctor sane and helps him deal with the anxieties of the patient.

So I feel now, when I lie in bed listening to Iris downstairs. Is it just another mode of self-protection? Or a symptom of fatigue. The less sleep I get nowadays the more capable I feel of displaying calmness and confidence. Unlike a true professional, a nurse or doctor, I am playing to an audience of one – myself. Iris is indifferent to my performance, and presumably unaware of it. I have to be my own audience; and giving a benefit of an audience of one is part of the solitude of this unchosen profession of carer.

I never minded sentry duty in the army. Two hours, four sometimes, in the middle of the night, gave one the chance to be away in some sense, although the need to keep alert made it hardly possible to daydream. Even when tired I never felt sleepy on those occasions, just as I don't now, when Iris is coming and going in the dim light, and building her mysterious heaps downstairs.

Suggestions that she should come to bed are not exactly ignored but as if put on a file for future reference. Quite courteously, her murmurings seem to imply that there are more important things to do before sleep can be thought of, and that in any case bed is now an unwelcome place, frequented too often and too long.

So Belial takes over, and my mind wanders off. Unlike on sentrygo, daydream seems the most natural state of mind when lying in bed. As a sentry in training one wandered rather as Iris is doing now, investigating shadows and corners but remaining in the open, so that one could be seen to be doing one's job if the officer came round. That at least was how it was at home, at Pirbright or Catterick. At the sharp end it was very different. There the sentry was concerned above all to remain invisible, so that if an enemy scout or raiding party were approaching they wouldn't see him first. The sentry's nightmare was to be stalked by such an enemy, and silently disposed of before he knew what was happening.

On army courses we were told that the Russians were specially good at such tactics. I wondered idly now whether Hannelore's fiancé had known all about that. I started remembering his cheerful ignorant face, so eerily untouched by what he must have gone through, and his dark unruly hair, so very unGerman, at least for those days.

Impossible somehow, although this must be just self-conceit again, to imagine him and Hannelore behaving like a married or an engaged couple; or talking at least as Hannelore and I used to talk on the sofa in the evenings. In the brief time I had seen them both together they appeared almost to avoid each other. Driving the Mercedes had seemed the peak of his enjoyment at being home after all those awful years.

Had those years been unremittingly so awful? – how could one know, since he said nothing? Or would he have woken up in the night with Hannelore, screaming from a nightmare, sobbing incoherently and beginning to tell her things? Somehow it was impossible to imagine that, which of course didn't mean it mightn't happen.

Another young German whom I met when out in T force and whom I plied with questions about the Russian front when I discovered he had been there, had not been at all reluctant to talk about it. On the contrary he was proud of having got through without a scratch, never anywhere near the enemy. He had been put in charge of some transport behind the lines, and had acquired a local *Bunkermädchen*, as he put it with coy facetiousness.

She kept him warm in bed and you needed it with the thermometer at forty below. What had happened to her in the retreat? He had no idea, nor was he in the least interested, but I was struck by the vehemence with which he disowned any idea that during the war he had done his duty for Germany and the *Führer*.

Perhaps Hannelore's fiancé had managed to find a *Bunkermädchen*, even in the Russian camps? Perhaps he, like the other, had good luck, the thing soldiers become aware of after the war, when they find not only that they are still alive but even have agreeable memories of those days. That happened not infrequently. With me he had been so amiable, and so totally incurious – would he be jealous and ask Hannelore about me afterwards; and would she tell him about other possible affairs of hers which I had known nothing of?

But I had, and still have, the feeling that all such things would be irrelevant to him. The past, which means everything now to me, was not going to exist for Hannelore and her new husband. Much better not, no doubt.

Back in England I felt too that it would be better to forget all about Germany, and the unsettling thoughts incurred by this brief revisitation. There were lots of other things that I must now try to do; I had my living to earn and my future to consider. Having taken my degree in 1950 at the mature age of twenty-five, I was now doing some teaching, but my position was a humble one and I had no secure job or means of support: the army indeed was still paying for my education.

Well-wishers advised me to embark on serious research for a higher degree. I could think of no one to work on except Sir Walter Scott, whom I liked for his approach to history and the past: I had lately much enjoyed reading him. But it is one thing to enjoy an author, quite another to 'work' on him: my affection for Scott languished when I had to visit libraries, look at manuscripts and read critical books. Like many authors who have to be worked on by students of Eng. Lit., Scott does not lend himself to the process. He should be read for himself, a quiet and mildly soporific turning of pages, at bedtime or teatime.

At this crucial period – the 'Shadow Line' as Conrad thought of it – when one is on the verge of the future and its yet unknown responsibilities, mere indolence is more tempting than any form of dissipation. I privately abandoned Scott as a subject, though I continued to read him as an author, and began to compose, as if in a dream, a novel about the time in Germany which was now over and done with. It came so easily: it was the perfect companion for indolence. It seemed to fill out mornings and evenings perfectly, almost as if I were reading Scott himself. I have never enjoyed doing anything more; and the new little foundation of St Antony's, where I was writing the novel at what seemed a soothing rate of between one and two thousand words a day, was the perfect place to be doing it in.

There were many stories about St Antony's, and much going on there under the counter, so to speak; but I knew nothing about such matters and they never disturbed my own tranquil existence in the little college. I had no duties or responsibilities other than 'helping' with the foreign students as a junior member of what was really an extended house party. St Antony's has since expanded and become a well-respected Centre of International Studies, but I feel it has never been more itself than in those early days, when about a dozen of us lived happily together in this former Anglican convent in the Woodstock Road, spartan within and drably Victorian without, and did our own things in harmonious privacy.

We did them under the command – St Antony's in early days always had a pleasantly if sometimes furtively military air about it – of Colonel Bill Deakin, who during the war had stood at Tito's side in many a tight corner during the guerilla war in Jugoslavia. And given him shrewd advice no doubt. Bill Deakin was small and wiry, very sharp but not frightening. He seemed to invite me to enjoy whatever mysterious game was going on without having to participate in it: he accepted my limitations with amusement and equanimity. It was all a bit like not being expected to play golf when I was a child, except that Bill Deakin was a much more genial figure than my father.

James Joll, his second-in-command, a jovial fair-haired Wykehamist with a curious bouncing walk, I had known when I was an undergraduate. Taking me aside one day he had said with an air of comic conspiracy, 'John, they are about to found a new college in order that I should be *Vice* Warden. Would you care to join us?'

His blue eyes twinkled in the kindliest way as he emphasised the word 'vice', but my own life at St Antony's was one of almost pastoral innocence. I suppose we did eat and drink rather a lot in the early days, and at a time when Oxford in general was still glumly undergoing the effects of wartime privation. We drank wine at all our meals like Frenchmen, because Antonin Besse, the potent figure who was our patron and founder, was indeed a Frenchman, a captain of commerce who had made his fortune along the Red Sea littoral – partly, it was hinted, by gun-running. He appears in a travel book by Evelyn Waugh, and had himself met Rimbaud when he was a very young man, somewhere in the wilds of Ethiopia. This fabulous figure had made no impression on Monsieur Besse, beyond the fact that he heard Rimbaud's trading ventures never came off. The poet-prodigy, who had abandoned the Muse at eighteen, and longed only to make money, was never much good at it apparently.

Monsieur Besse, who was rumoured to have found Oxford graduates particularly promising material as entrepreneurs in dubious projects, used periodically to descend on his fief to see how things were going. One graduate from the college who was recruited in this way into his business empire also became his son-in-law. Did he know about the other activity of St Antony's in its earliest phase? – recruitment not of spies exactly, but of intellectuals for the fringes of Whitehall security organisations? I know next to nothing about it myself, and knew nothing then, but I used to enjoy talking to David Footman, a sardonic avuncular person who wrote books about Russia and communism and was often away on government business. The higher echelons of St Antony's always had the air of being up to things they did not talk about.

I remained at St Anthony's for three or four years, greatly enjoying both the sociable side of the college and its convent-like seclusion, in which I could happily live while trying to write my novel. In the evenings Dr Zaehner, an expert on oriental religions, taught us to play backgammon, which he called 'tric-trac'. I never understood it properly but I loved to hear Robin Zaehner's manic giggle as he manoeuvred the pieces, chatting the while about Ormuzd and Ahriman and the legendary Zoroaster.

When Monsieur Besse came to visit we were paraded for his inspection. Looking and sounding just like my idea of Napoleon he would examine and address us in turn, barking out *'Et que faites-vous ici?'* with genial ferocity. It was hard to keep any aplomb with him; and when I somehow got out, in bad French, that I taught English literature, he shrugged immensely and turned up his eyes in mock despair. Obviously he expected more enterprise than that. But he did not seem to hold it too much against me, and while he was in the college we all wined and dined in our best country-house-party style.

Naturally enough the novel turned out to be all about Germany, and in a sense about Hannelore too, though there was a good deal else that I made up, including the plot. At the end of it the young hero, demobilised as I had been, and out of a job, has a phone call from the girl – she is called Lise – whom he left in Germany. She has managed to come over to England and is ringing from London, from Harrods. As a child I thought Harrods the most romantic place in the world, which must have been why I chose it for this reunion.

About this time, Michael Jaffé, a brilliant sardonic art critic who looked like an Assyrian monarch on a bas-relief and whom I had known at school, asked me in the kindest and most flattering manner what I was working on. When he heard that it was a novel, and that the hero and heroine were reunited at the end in Harrods, he burst into guffaws of laughter. He was driving me to Cambridge at that moment for a college feast, and his mirth became so uncontrollable that he was compelled to pull into the side of the road and stop the car until it subsided.

I was genuinely puzzled by his response, though gratified too, because it seemed to show that the novel was funnier than I realised. That must be all to the good, no matter how unintentional in this case the humour might be. Why Harrods should have struck him in this context as so hilarious I still cannot fathom, but alas he is dead and I cannot ask him. I told him I thought of calling the novel *In Another Country*. Ah yes, he said knowledgeably. Marlowe – *Jew of Malta* (he was Jewish himself) – '*But that was in another country, and besides, the wench is dead.*'

I recalled the quotation, memorably used by T.S. Eliot as an epigraph for one of his poems, but it hadn't occurred to me when I thought of a title. In my sentimental vision the wench, Lise, was very much alive, and had come to find her lover in England, sure that he still needed her. I felt he did too.

Lise looked a bit like Hannelore of course, but she was much more loving, more mature, more masterful. A daydream in fact. And yet as I wrote I kept remembering that puzzled lost bewildered look on Hannelore's face when I'd had enough, and told her I must go because my brother needed the car. A look of child-like disappointment, and something more too, as if she had inconveniently found herself committed to an old lover when a more recent one had just come back to her.

The real Hannelore must have been very different. I don't doubt that. But daydreams feed on such sudden unexpected looks on familiar faces, faces with which one can imagine oneself in love.

And scarcely was the novel finished before I had another face to dream about, an image which instantly dispelled my tranquil time in what had once been the nunnery of St Antony's. The new face had come from a nunnery itself, as it happened, but its owner had finally been rejected as a postulant, and had come out again, however reluctantly, into the world. As soon as I saw that face I felt myself to be seriously in love.

It had all come from a poem I had seen in an old-fashioned green-covered monthly called *The Countryman*, which my parents took at home. I liked *The Countryman* anyway, and this poem, 'Evening Primrose', seemed to me then, as it still does, exceptional and charming. In a sort of amateurish footnote, typical of *The Countryman*'s lack of pretension, the editor had mentioned that the author of the poem repaired fine china for a living in a small Cotswold town. I wrote on impulse to the address to say how much I had enjoyed the poem, and a correspondence began. Eventually we met, the town not being far from Oxford.

Mary was a good bit older than I, with hair beginning

to be touched with grey at the temples. She was shy in manner and had an enchanting smile, as many nuns or ex-nuns have, which lit up the whole of her face. In repose her face had a resigned and sad look which seemed its natural expression.

In the bus on the way back to Oxford I kept telling myself that if the bus reached a set of traffic lights before they turned red, or if the driver managed to get up a hill without changing gear, then she would marry me. I usually won this game, no doubt because I had subconsciously worked out the odds before making the bet with myself. As the vehicle ground the last few yards into the bus station I put all my winnings on a man who stood on its rear platform with umbrella and briefcase, obviously late for some appointment and impatient to get off. If he did so before the bus came to a stop then I would have scooped the pool, and our marriage was a certainty. Of course he did, sprinting lightly away towards the High Street, but I walked slowly back to St Antony's without any feeling of exultation: only a great and as it seemed a meaningless anxiety.

I had won my bet, and yet in the same moment part of me knew it meant nothing, except – oddly enough – that I was not really in love with Mary at all. I was really just imagining how delightful, how magical, it would be if I were.

And yet during the next few weeks I sincerely wished I had never met this woman. Like Gretchen at her spinning wheel my *Ruhe* was *hin* and my *Herz* was *schwer*. The delightful tranquillity of St Antony days, in which I had seemed to be waiting contentedly and without curiosity for the next thing to happen, was now a thing of the past. I seemed to be writing Mary a continuous love-letter, to which I received disappointingly meagre and politely baffled replies.

Persistence eventually made me at least familiar to her. Though she lived a reclusive life in the Cotswold bedsitter, surrounded by bits of china under repair, she was prepared to come to Oxford now and again. We sat in my cell at St Antony's – it seemed a suitable background for her – drinking wine and eating Marks and Spencer sandwiches. We talked about literature and poetry and that sort of thing, stiltedly and self-consciously as it seemed to me, but I found no way of making our conversation happy and spontaneous.

She seemed painfully unused to talking, but to enjoy it none the less as a new way of coming to terms with secular life. Although she loved discussing books and poems I didn't enjoy it at all: every word seemed to push us apart and make her quite different from the woman I had first seen, as from the woman who had written the Evening Primrose poem.

Our only good moments, as it seemed to me, came in the summer evenings – it was now June – when I went back home with her on the bus. We used to get off it in the country and walk the last mile or two in the summer twilight. Once we saw an owl sitting motionless on a telegraph pole beside the road. Displaying what knowledge I possessed, gratuitously as usual, I told her Hegel's comment about the owl of wisdom, Minerva's bird, only taking its flight in the evening. Presumably because it was by then too late for wise counsels to come to the aid of mankind and to save the world? At such moments Mary had a rather annoying habit of looking indulgent while ignoring what was being said. She continued to gaze at the bird in silence until it grew self-conscious in its turn and drifted away into the dusk like a shadow.

I thought of telling Mary about my owl at the ruined cottage on Romney Marsh. I was about speak but decided with satisfaction not to. I would keep all such things to and for myself, for I was aware of feeling, with an even greater flood of satisfaction, that I was really beginning to fall out of love with Mary. But I had already started to make the first sounds of confiding my owl story, and to my amazement I heard myself say instead, 'I do wish you would marry me.'

Mary came to an abrupt halt. We stood there on the road in the tepid darkness, gazing at the white blur of each other's face. My unexpected words had filled me with consternation but now I felt calm, almost uninterested. The ball was in Mary's court. I waited with mild curiosity to see how she would play it.

She didn't. She simply walked on in silence, leaving me beginning to feel both silly and tiresome. Also impertinent. In silence we walked on into the little town, and to the point of the street where we usually said goodnight, Mary being unwilling that we should approach together the small house in which she lodged. We stopped, and I was about to say goodnight and escape when Mary seized me by the arm – we had no previous physical contact – and started to walk me rapidly back to the place where we had seen the owl sitting on the telegraph pole.

[171]

Arrived there she swung me towards her and kissed me on the mouth.

If Hannelore's kisses had been like a good ping-pong player deftly returning the little ball, Mary's was like something she had read about and suddenly received a chance to try out in action. It was more of a buffet than a kiss, and her lips were cool and dry like paper. After administering it she stood back, and dark as it was now growing I could see she was looking at me intently.

'Do you really mean that?' she asked. 'Because of course, if you do, I am going to say yes.'

In contrast to the look on her face the voice she spoke in was low and urgent, although it still had something of the quiet unworldly sardonic tone which seemed to me to go with the face for which I loved her. It was capable of such swift gentleness and intimacy, and yet at the same time was so austere and far away. Now that I seemed almost painfully close to the two of them, face and voice together, I was paralysed and wholly bereft of initiative. I could only stutter something vaguely, and she paid no attention.

Taking my arm again she said, 'Well let's just walk about a bit until we've calmed down.'

We did that. As we walked I began to recover something of my talkativeness. I embraced her and we stopped and kissed every few yards. I had scarcely been conscious of her body before, indeed hardly knew she had one, for the kind of garments she wore seemed to remove from her any feminine reality. Now I explored her with growing ardour, though decorously too. She ignored what I was doing and did not respond to it, but she began to talk with a quite unusual vivacity. We laughed, still in a rather brittle way, but with an increasing sense of relaxation between us.

I assured her – what else could I do? – that of course I had meant it. I longed to marry her. I began to talk about what we would do, where we would live. She only half listened, I felt, though she continued to smile almost ecstatically at me as we kissed. I could not make out whether she was simply indulging the antics of her admirer, or whether I had said something for which she had been waiting – could that possibly be it? – but which, now it had come, she did not none the less take quite seriously, or indeed know what to do about.

But between these alternatives I did not feel in the least upset or tantalised. Both seemed to me equally marvellous, equally full of a kind of onrushing and intoxicating promise. What did it matter if she didn't know what line to take, what to think of this new development? I didn't know either. The wonderful thing was that we had achieved a new kind of relationship, and if it had let me in for a permanent future with Mary, then so be it.

Being married to her seemed easily imaginable, delightfully and soberly alluring. I imagined Mary's face beside my own in the church, and friends and relatives looking at us admiringly, and sitting together in our garden when someone, perhaps the vicar, had dropped in to tea. Imagination could do much: all it failed to do was to see what life after marriage would really be like.

That did not matter. The fresh wild pleasure of our nocturnal walk was everything. We patrolled that road, far back out into the country, and when in the silence of the summer night we heard a stream close by we managed to get through a fence and find it. Flowing water glimmered in the obscurity, and we crouched down at the edge and joined hands together under the water. I babbled about this being a pagan or pantheistic betrothal. Mary said nothing, only laughing a little in her old quiet way, but she kissed me again and again.

Now, nearly fifty years later, I have inclination and time – time in my own mind at least – to wonder what she meant, and what she made of it all. Were she as clueless as I was, even though in a different, older, more essentially melancholy way, she must also have been just as confused, just as incapable of knowing or controlling what was happening.

Or was the matter, at least for her that evening, both more trivial and more easily foreseen and taken care of? Had I, almost inadvertently, started a play in which it was a pleasure and even a delight to perform? I remember thinking, with a qualm of depression but also a sneaking sense of relief, that neither of us could be quite serious about the way we were behaving: the only serious thing was our sense of liberation – and clearly we were both feeling that – into the joyfulness of being together, and talking and kissing in the way that we were.

Otherwise? – well. Was Mary herself entranced – liberated too – by the happy way we were both playing our parts while she was receiving, possibly for the first time, a proposal of marriage? In those days such a proposal, no matter how made or by whom, was quite something. Thinking about it all these many years later I can imagine

Mary saying to a friend, 'Well, you know, there *was* this young man, in those days, who wanted to marry me' – and she would be saying it with the gentle half-sardonic smile I still remember so well. Perhaps it would be something she had made a poem about, like the one on the Evening Primrose.

In fact I did spot some years later, and not in *The Countryman*, which I no longer saw at my parents' home, but in the much glossier and more prestigious magazine *Country Life*, a poem by Mary about the owl sitting on the telegraph pole. It was a good poem, rather in the manner of Mary Coleridge, the great STC's collateral descendant, and it showed the same art in producing a tension between a natural object closely observed, and an emotional situation which was not specified.

I had not given a thought to Mary for ages and had lost all touch with her, but on reading the poem I at once felt a kind of jealousy and annoyance, as if a possession of my own had been taken and used without leave. Highly unfair, because Mary too had seen the owl just as I had, and yet I felt a grievance none the less, although I did cut out the poem and keep it.

It was above seven in the evening when we had reached the outskirts of the little town after our walk from the bus. By the time Mary disentwined herself from me and said she really must be going in, it was well past midnight. At intervals during our feverishly happy chatter, which came much more from me than from her, I had used phrases like 'When we are married,' 'Where shall we have the wedding?' and 'Where shall we go for our honeymoon?'

To none of this did Mary make any reply; but that did not seem to matter in the least, perhaps not to either of us; although after some hours I think both of us had unconsciously had enough. Mary enquired, rather unromantically I thought, if I was hungry. I discovered that I was, but I said no, of course not, and on that note we parted. I watched Mary turn a key and silently enter the little house where she lived. She turned and waved, and I waved back deliriously before setting out on the two mile walk back to the main road.

The evening's adventures were not yet over. I intended to hitch a lift back to Oxford, something I had often done before and which in those days presented no sort of problem. It was a moonless night but I got up to the big road without difficulty and stood waiting for the headlights of the long-distance lorries that drove by from Wales and from the Bristol docks. One rumbled into view at last and looked like stopping for me, but as I ran up the road to scramble into the cab it accelerated again and its red tail light vanished in the darkness. There was another close behind it which did stop at the sight of my gesticulating figure, and I thanked the driver effusively as he re-engaged the gears of his big Leyland Octopus – I still remember the type of the lorry and the cargo of tobacco it was carrying. It was restful not being able to talk above the roar of the engine housed between driver and passenger, and I was nearly asleep when the lorry stopped with a sudden jerk. Ahead was the lorry that had nearly stopped for me – I recognised the white-painted name on the tailboard – stationary and evidently in collision with another vehicle.

My driver scrambled out and I followed him. There was a great cloud of blue dust in the air, evidently from the cargo of one of the wrecked lorries, and there was already a considerable crowd about, moving and gesticulating agitatedly through a thick blue fog stabbed with headlights. My driver was talking and shouting to some others, and through the pulverised windscreen of the lorry that had been ahead of us I could make out hands, very white, splayed against the ruin as if a part of it.

My driver turned abruptly and went back to his cab, with me following. 'Done for. Fell asleep I reckon,' was all he said as we scrambled in. There were no seat belts in those days. As if still in a sinister dream I jumped off when my driver stopped for me at the Woodstock crossroads – no roundabout then – and remembered to shout up my thanks. He was away without further comment, no doubt keen to get the load to London and be off home, and I began to walk slowly down the dark empty road into Oxford.

Halfway there I made out a tall figure in the gloom on the opposite pavement, who began to cross the road purposefully towards me. One had not the least fear or even an awareness of muggers in those days – in 1952 such things just did not happen – and in any case I soon made out the policeman's helmet. He strolled up to me in leisurely fashion. 'Out a bit late, lad, aren't you?' he observed, without seeming to expect an answer.

I at once felt greatly relieved, not by what he said but

by his general demeanour in the faint light that was beginning to dawn. Everything, I felt, would now be all right, including of course my marriage to Mary, which had become rather lost sight of in the recent events on the road.

I remembered what was supposed to be a chilling moment in one of Sax Rohmer's Fu Manchu stories, which I had been fond of when young. The heroine, escaping and pursued by sinister and silent Chinamen, looks wildly round for help as she runs along a dark road. 'But there was no one in sight, not even a policeman'. Clearly policemen were as common as lamp-posts in those days.

The recollection was interrupted by my own policeman interrupting his air of peaceful scrutiny to ask what I had in that bag. I usually had a book or two which I had lent to Mary, who was scrupulous about returning such things, and I hastened to produce these for the policeman's inspection.

Satisfied, he turned away with a pacific, 'Good morning, Sir,' and I went on my way down to St Antony's, comforted by the encounter, though for the next day or so I often thought about the poor truck-driver's bloodless hands.

Before I went to bed I started to write a love-letter. Although I had thought of the previous ones as love-letters they were really just intended to sparkle and to impress. I found the authentic thing extraordinarily hard to do: and abandoning it at about six in the morning fell immediately and very deeply asleep.

For the next twenty-four hours I knew that something

of vital importance had occurred and that my whole life would have to be changed. But I had trouble remembering what the thing was. Another thing in me didn't want to remember. The novel was finished, and so in a sense I was at a loose end; and yet I had never before felt so comfortable in my burrow-like routines at St Antony's. My bit of teaching in the mornings, the cinema perhaps in the afternoon; at night reading in my room, after college dinner and perhaps a game of tric-trac or draughts with Dr Zaehner. How had it happened that all this should have been put under threat? I had some serious disease, and been given only months or weeks to live.

I had lately been reading the philosopher Wittgenstein: everyone was doing it. Along with A.J. Ayer's *Language, Truth and Logic* his *Tractatus* was all the rage. Without understanding much of it I enjoyed the simplicity and confidence of the style. I had been especially struck by one calm observation: something about the different worlds we live in, and the world of the healthy being quite different from that of the sick.

I knew now just what he meant. Something had gone seriously wrong inside me. The events of last night were not going to go away. They meant I was in love, and had entered a different world, one quite unlike the little St Antony's world of my own, which I could so happily control. In the course of the day I finished my love-letter as if I were making a will, and sent it off.

Two mornings later I scrabbled feverishly in my pigeon-hole. If there had been no letter from Mary I should have been desolated, as well as deeply wounded. But there was a letter. Up in my little nun's cell I tore it open.

I somehow knew it would be gentle, a bit constrained, considerate for me. It would perhaps be better not to meet, at least not just yet. She would always treasure our talks together and my kindness about her poems – the way I had written about 'Evening Primrose' . . .

The letter, opening with 'Dear John', did indeed begin with thanks. It had been a lovely day, and she did so hope I had got back safely? I put the letter down, with a leaden sense of disappointment, even misery. I looked at the books on the desk and on my bed. None of them held the slightest interest for me now. Neither did the last pages of the novel, laboriously typed, arranged neatly and waiting to be corrected. Listlessly I picked up the letter again. Mary's writing was neat too, without being in any way fancy, and perfectly easy to read. But after a sort of hiatus near the bottom of the first page it started off again in a much wilder script, almost illegible. Sitting down I started to concentrate.

She loved me – she wanted me – she longed to marry me. She wanted me for her very own. No matter for God, the Church, her life, her poems – anything else. She loved me. Would I really marry her? Would I come to her, please?

The letter was quite short – a single page and the reverse not even completed, or signed. My own had of course been much longer.

I was already in a fever of departure, putting on my coat, a tie. I ran down to the bicycle shed – there could be no question of waiting for a bus. Within a few minutes of opening the letter I was bicycling out of Oxford.

It was a hot day and a long way, with a lot of hills. I

had plenty of time to reflect on what I was doing, and on my own astonishment at doing it at all. But I knew I must do it. I knew, or at least I had read somewhere, that the fulfilment of sexual obsession is like a dreadful duty. But whatever demon was driving me now it was not sex. I did not really desire Mary: I was still barely aware of her as a woman. Why then?

By now I was so hot and uncomfortable, in imminent danger too from passing lorries whose slipstream nearly knocked me off my bike, that I ceased to feel any interest in why I was doing it. The great thing was to get there.

And eventually I did. I had never been inside the house; it was the first time I had knocked on the door. It was opened by a rather disagreeable-looking woman with a pursed-up mouth. She glowered at me. I explained I wanted to see Mary, and the woman reluctantly let me go up the cramped cottage stairs. I was aware of her standing at the bottom and eyeing me. I knocked on a door.

Mary jumped up awkwardly, almost knocking over a piece of china under repair. She did not seem pleased to see me. There was no telephone of course; I could not have rung Mary up, but it occurred to me that it might have been wiser as well as more civil to have sent a telegram, a 'wire' as they were known in those days. It also occurred to me, and with a definite pang, that if I had my snug little burrow at St Antony's, so had Mary her own out here, one which she must need and want as much as I did mine.

Mary's face looked pinched, and her mouth as pursed-up as that of her landlady. She also seemed flustered

[181]

and embarrassed, even frightened. My discomfort was extreme, and before anything was said I realised that others beside myself had daydreams and desires and vague longings which they neither wished nor expected to be implemented and put into action. Mary had written a letter – the second half of it – on the peak of one of those. And now here I was, rudely butting in on her own life, a life which she cherished in her own way as much as I did mine.

I was right of course. Mary became very quiet and calm. She asked me to forget about the letter. A little more experience might have told me that something here was seriously amiss, but I was much too concerned with my own feelings. The things that had charmed me about Mary – a smile, her good sense, her touching interest in everything I talked about and told her – were ways of guarding and protecting something deeply disturbed within. Her poems, her devotions, her meticulous work with china, were doing the same.

She seemed frank about this. She told me she had yielded to some silly irrational impulse, and now she must frighten me off for my own good. So please go.

But I at once determined not to be frightened off. As I bicycled slowly back to Oxford – more than twenty miles and it seemed to take me the rest of the day – I resolved whatever happened to hang on. She had changed her mind once: why shouldn't she change it again? – and for good this time?

It was a hope born of ignorance and disregard rather than of innocence. Not only was my idea of marriage – Mary beside me in a white wedding-dress, and the vicar coming to tea – wholly ridiculous, but I was self-ish enough to suppose that Mary must have the same delightful view of it, if indeed I bothered to think of her having any view at all.

What mattered was that she had said she loved me and wanted me. *Wanted* me – above all. It was that word, rather than love, which so deeply moved and flattered me.

I knew every word of that part of her letter by heart, and repeated them like a charm as I bicycled along in a state of near exhaustion. I had been so frightened bicycling out on the main road – this was long before the days of dual carriageways and cycle-paths – that I returned to Oxford along a devious route through the country lanes, getting lost in the process and adding miles to the journey.

The next day I heard from Mary again. It was an affectionate quiet letter, merely saying she did hope we might go on seeing each other as before. The tone of this letter annoyed as well as depressed me. So Mary merely wanted to go on making use of me as a pal, to borrow books and to chat about poetry and so forth? Well, thank you very much. Just as I had absolutely believed the words which said she loved and wanted me, so I now believed a friendly letter which said couldn't we be friends? It never occurred to me that Mary, who was after all nearly ten years older than I was, could be a victim of love's uncertain madness to an extent which made my own feelings look solipsistic, as well as jejune. She was the real Gretchen at the spinning wheel, whose peace and quiet I had in a sense quite thoughtlessly destroyed.

Looking back, something I have hardly done till now – this moment when memory has assumed the paramount place in consciousness – it looks as if I fell in love with Mary because she was not tough: did not have, that is to say, a normal feminine degree of resilience, of wiry and wary calculation. I may have unconsciously intuited that, and it may have made a strong hidden appeal.

Mary was defenceless. Not in the sense that she could be taken advantage of sexually: I had no idea how to set about that, and no wish to do it either. She had wanted earlier to give herself to God, or to Christ, a need so incomprehensible to me that I could not even begin to imagine it. Had I accidentally given her the impulse to want me instead, or at least want something beyond a quiet life repairing china, going to church and seeing a circle of friends?

Thinking of the owl on the telegraph pole, which Mary was later to write a poem about, reminds me by association how owlish it must always be to write down one's own love experiences. They may seem interesting to me now, but when they happened they were just like everyone else's experiences. Sex may be the ever interesting topic, but love is interesting only to oneself, which is why it seems owlish to expatiate upon it publicly. (Incidentally why should the owl, Minerva's bird, be an emblem of wisdom, when to be owlish is to be merely obtuse, if not downright stupid?)

I was still fixated about Mary. Had she written, 'I'm sorry but I never want to see you again', I should not, I think, have persevered. A dramatic rejection would have satisfied me and set my feelings as much in a proper groove as a joyful acceptance would have done. The awareness of this was what annoyed me, and yet I had the sense to realise that my own best interests – at least as I then saw them – lay in going along with what she had suggested.

So she came to see me again in St Antony's, though I did not now go back home with her to the town where she lived. We sat in my bedsitter as before and had a sandwich and a glass of white wine and talked about books. Should she read Chaucer, *The Faerie Queen*? . . . We debated the question while boredom mounted up in my heart and soul. There were occasional animated moments when Mary seemed to forget herself. Looking suddenly into my eyes she would say, 'John – if only we *could* get married . . .' Like a hunter not daring to move for fear of disturbing shy game, I would remain silent, only returning her look. The next day I would get a brief letter saying, 'Dear John, I am sorry that I am me'.

It turned cold early in December and there was snow even in Oxford. Feeling suddenly resolved I hastened down to the bus station. In the country the snow was thick. I seemed to wade through it to Mary's door. Mary was sitting idly in her tiny room. There were no bits of china under repair. Last time there had been drafts of a poem scattered about, but now there was nothing.

In the bus I had let myself imagine her springing up with a cry, flinging her arms tightly round me and saying, 'Oh, I'm so glad you've come.' I could hear her saying it, and so clearly that when I stood before her I thought for a second she was saying it. But the chilly room remained silent, snow-muffled. Mary's face looked puffy and unusually pale, though in comparison with Hannelore it had never looked exactly rubicund.

When she spoke at last her voice sounded clogged and peevish. 'I warn you I'm getting a cold,' she said. 'So am I,' I replied, which was true enough. 'Don't worry.'

There seemed nothing else to say. She looked away from me towards the window. I had the feeling she was on the verge of tears: also that she was glad I had come, despite appearances; but this feeling gave me neither hope nor pleasure. At the same time I felt I had never loved her more than as she looked now, plain and disreputable, with the grey in her hair much in evidence. For the first time I really desired her. I longed to take her in my arms and make love to her, even though I had very little idea how this should be done when it came to the homely details; and I knew that Mary had no idea either: I could not expect any help from her.

The fact somehow made me so woebegone that I felt tears coming into my eyes. Then I saw that hers had them too. We began to smile at each other in a way that was almost amused and apologetic. I had never shed tears with anyone before, and the sensation it gave was extraordinarily comforting, even exhilarating. In a minute or two we were chatting quite normally. Mary said she would make some tea. She had to leave the room to do this and I heard a murmur of voices below as if she was continuing her own life, which had been going quietly on before mine, and would continue to do so after I had disappeared and been forgotten.

The thought made me so forlorn again that I could not smile or say anything when Mary reappeared. We seemed to be just on the edge of a wonderful moment which would change our lives but which both of us knew would never happen. We drank the tea in silence, and I still remember how weak and disagreeable it was. Should we always be drinking such nasty tea if we got married? The thought amused and cheered me somewhat; and I was aware, too, that my agonised impression that we were just on the edge of delirious happiness, if we could only nerve ourselves to reach it, was a scene I had picked up from the cinema and from books. Probably a story by Chekhov?

'What are you smiling at?' said Mary, slightly peevish again. I did not tell her, but I think she understood, and was hurt a little. There seemed nothing I could do about that now, nothing to comfort her, though I still longed to do so by some physical means.

'We are rather like a Victorian couple in a novel, aren't we?' I found myself saying instead. Mary seemed to have this effect on me, and I remembered the moment when I had found myself saying, in equally casual terms, something about our getting married.

Mary looked hard and cold now. The emotions of the last few minutes seemed to have vanished away pathetically, knowing they were no use. 'When's your bus?' she asked. I told her the time of the next one back and she said she would come with me to the bus-stop. I besought her not to, with her cold coming on, but she took no notice. Fortunately there was not long to wait and we talked as much as we could. She asked about my plans and my teaching. She seemed like an aunt inquiring about a nephew's future; but I realised she was distrait and not interested in what I said.

The bus came, churning up the unexpected snow which was still dazzling white in its headlights. I got on and sat stiffly at the back. There was an interminable wait while the driver conferred with some unseen person outside his window. Then at my own window Mary's face suddenly appeared, gazing at me, as it seemed imploringly. I got up in haste, but at that moment the driver engaged gear and we lunged heavily away up the hill.

My sore throat was now painful enough to occupy most of my attention. I felt feverish, and the cold was really coming on. But I remembered that a friend who was already a fellow of Lincoln College and Tutor in English had asked me to a party in his rooms that evening, a Saturday. William Empson, a great name and a legendary figure in our Eng. Lit. world at that time, was going to be there.

I went, drank as much as I could, and fell off my bicycle in the snow at two a.m. on my way back to St Antony's. But I had met a couple who knew someone I had known in Gerrards Cross. More important they had been going to bring a friend of theirs whom they said they would have liked me to meet. She had cried off at the last moment because of a former entanglement with our host, whom she did not now wish to encounter. They did not mention her name, but that was the first time I heard of the existence of Iris.

I had a letter from Mary the following day saying please,

she did not want to see me again. There was silence until nine or ten years later; although I heard from an acquaintance that she had later on been through a bad time, even – the friend thought – an attempted suicide, but was now fully recovered. Then Mary herself wrote out of the blue. She was living in a different place, further from Oxford, but she did so hope that my wife and I might be able to visit them.

The invitation came again and eventually we went to a lunch which I recall as being painfully vegetarian. Mary was living with a woman friend, to whom she seemed to be in a state of total subordination. I suspected this friend might have made Mary ask us out of curiosity. Neither Iris nor I took to her at all. Such instant hostility was rare indeed on the part of Iris, who was never in the least censorious or critical. But the woman's attempts to silence Mary, whom Iris took to at once, and to block off her timid friendliness and her equally timid attempts to ask about Plato and the Christian mystics – all this upset Iris and annoyed her even more. The lunch was not a success, nor was it repeated.

The friend abandoned Mary soon after, and a convent near Worcester took her in for a while. She remained in correspondence with Iris until her death, and in this way became a 'pal for life'. That was how another fan of Iris once expressed it when Iris had replied sympathetically and thoughtfully to her letters.

10

'Thou met'st with things dying, I with things newborn'. It happens to me nowadays to be haunted by Shakespeare's line, which suggests that the two states are not so very different. Sometimes Iris's resemblance to a three-year-old is so uncanny that I find myself expecting her to shrink to an appropriate size.

My own enactment of a parent's role is equally exact, involuntarily faithful. Sometimes when I give her supper with a spoon Iris will eat her creamed rice or baked beans with a sort of negligent greed, like a child pretending it doesn't really want them, is above such things as food. More often she turns her head away, and yet when I proffer a spoonful opens her mouth obediently at once, like a chick on the nest. Being fed is still a pleasure to her.

'Bed now?' I say hopefully but she doesn't care for the idea, or for any other course of action. She sits, and when I smile at her smiles back as if she knows perfectly well what I have in mind.

What I have in mind is my own drink and supper, my own blessed hour when the children are safe in bed, and the parents can relax with each other and resume adult life and its pleasures. At least I would suppose

JOHN BAYLEY

that is what they would do, and would feel like. But I am a lone parent, as they are called today; and I should imagine that a lone parent's evening relaxation, solitary as it may be, provides an even sharper and sweeter relief than those in a communal family.

I don't feel like a father and I don't feel like a mother either: I'm just going through the joint parental struggles, trials and compensations. Not rewards, because rewards would be seeing the kiddies growing up and saying new words and all the rest of it.

But I do fully appreciate the compensations. And I have that eerie feeling, when Iris smiles back at me as if she knew how much I am going to enjoy my drink when she is in bed, that she is herself cheered and supported by an awareness of the compensations I am getting.

It can hardly be so, yet it certainly feels like it. Three-year-olds don't care whether their parents are enjoying themselves or not. But perhaps they just assume they are, and that is much the same thing?

I don't know how it is with three-year-olds, but Iris's toilet habits, if you can call them that, have become unpredictable. Sometimes she will go to the right place, even though she makes a mess of it. More often she will do it on the carpet outside, or in another room. Then she lays the results, as if with care, on a neighbouring chair or bookshelf. I don't mind a bit cleaning up, an operation which seems mildly to amuse her. I can make a joke of it too, and we can laugh about it together. A small domestic challenge I can easily meet, and Iris seems to enjoy seeing me do it.

Certainly she can now have childish pleasures, presumably undreamt of before. Like the fingernail cutting. I take her arm firmly under mine so that she is behind me, her head laid shrinkingly against my back. She jibs and starts as I carefully cut the nails, with little shrieks and intakes of breath as if she were sure I am going to hurt her. But I can feel she is enjoying it really – the fearful joy of a child.

Time for bed at last. I've given her the sleeping-draught disguised as a 'drink'. Mango and orangeade, a few drops of sweet Cyprus wine. Unlike the Promazine this stuff smells nasty by itself and presumably tastes so too, but Iris drinks it quite happily in its juicy form. All through supper she has been hugging an old summer dress she has found somewhere. Now she goes up the stairs trailing it behind her, looking exactly like E.H. Shepard's illustration to *Winnie the Pooh*. Christopher Robin going up the stairs, dragging Pooh behind him.

I settle Iris down, turn her over, kiss her goodnight. I turn the light off and promise to leave the passage light on. Then I go quietly downstairs, but not yet to my drink. Like every other parent no doubt, I know what may happen. Usually it does. No noise, just a face looking round the door. 'You'll catch cold – back to bed with you at once.' (We used to call it 'mat', from an earlier pretence that we were cats: but now we have reverted to the normal use of bed, the thing that children go up to.)

It may happen again – probably will. Then there is peace at last, total quiet, except for the subdued music of my radio. I pour out my own drink with loving care. But

[193]

before tasting it I tiptoe upstairs, listen for a few seconds. Still all quiet. I look in very cautiously. Not a sound. Iris's head sideways on the pillow. The light from the door just shows her face, calm and relaxed, as if Dr Alzheimer had sent a friend to soothe away the daytime fears of a consciousness without speech or understanding.

Going down I can almost hear myself saying to an invisible, unknowable co-parent, 'All OK. She's dropped off.'

What would I do without her? Impossible now to imagine any other routine. I certainly cannot imagine enjoying my solitary drink unless Iris was safely in bed and asleep upstairs. When she has to go . . . If I can find somewhere to take her . . . At first only for a few days? But I want the present life, the present stage, to go on for ever.

Do parents feel like that sometimes, about their children? Surely not? Yet to lose a child must be the worst thing of all? Just because they are such a blessed nuisance?

After nearly fifty years I feel far closer to Iris than a parent could be to a child. A child, however loved and doted on, is still 'a little stranger'. Every day the knowledge that Iris and I are one flesh grows more overwhelming. The further the illness takes her away in the spirit, the more she is with me in the flesh.

Were she to be in a home, however 'happy' they would try to make her, the sense of apartness would soon destroy us both. Perhaps me before her, perhaps her before me? At the moment she keeps me sane. The final egoism is it? What would happen to me if she weren't here? Is that my real fear?

*   *   *

When his wife went off her head Macbeth expected the same things from his doctor that we hope for from ours today.

> Can'st thou not minister to a mind diseased?
> Pluck from the memory a rooted sorrow . . .

I fancy that the doctor may have tried on his royal patient all the somnolent potions that were at his command, although he tells Macbeth, perhaps defensively, that the patient must 'minister to himself' when it comes to staying sane and getting a good night's rest.

Sedatives are tricky things. Lady Macbeth's sleep-walking and her hallucinations could easily be the consequence of some too strenuous type of soporific. Chloral used to do it, if regularly taken. Rossetti died of it; and that was what was the matter with Evelyn Waugh when he had the experiences which led him to write that remarkable book, *The Ordeal of Gilbert Pinfold*.

In the early stages of Alzheimer's Iris never needed a sleeping-pill at all. She slept easily, both all night and in the afternoon, sometimes dozing in the morning as well. That lucky gift has now abandoned her. She goes to sleep like a child still, but in the night other things happen. Waking up I know at once she is no longer there. With an uncharacteristically stealthy movement she has gone from beside me, while I still slept. Now I lie tense and listening as on that night when it first occurred. The house is wholly quiet; I can see the light from the weak bulb in the passageway. Not a sound, but then suddenly I hear, and much more often now, the voice which doesn't sound like Iris saying quite clearly, 'Who is it? Who is it?' and then 'Hullo, hullo, are you there?'

It has become just like that Walter de la Mare story of the old man who walks about the house in the small hours, saying with querulous patience, 'Coming, coming.'

I look at my watch. Half-past two. I make a quick calculation: which potion to give her now? Sometimes it is better to wait. Iris may come back, led like a moth by the bedside light I've switched on. She will get quietly into bed, and we will make happy normal noises together as she nestles down.

But if nothing happens for a longish time I have to go in search of her. She is usually standing quietly in a room, having switched the light on. She smiles at me; we greet each other almost like two guests at a party. I take her hand and try to lead her back to the bedroom; but sometimes she resists quietly, turns in the opposite direction, stumbles up or down the stairs, evading me. It may seem best to leave her then. It is no use my going back to bed, but I go through the motions, hoping to lure her to follow me. Sometimes she does, but more often not. The impulses, whatever they are, have to work themselves out, and then she will come back, and sleep when daylight begins to show.

Going about the house after her in the dead of the night makes me also remember Henry James and Rye: that time we were there in his house. For me now Iris is like an elusive Muse, a Muse who has to be coaxed, cosseted, rescued from herself. Why should I think of

Henry James doing such a thing, but somehow it seems appropriate. Women did inspire him after all, and then by making much of them he kept them from coming too close. Iris, in this ghostly non-time, can seem concerned I should not come too close to her. She has been calling out in the motionless house for someone else. For whom?

For whom does she cry out *'Are you there?'* and demand *'Who is it?'* Is it her own vanished Muse?

The sadness of it all, the sadness I thought I felt in Lamb House at Rye, when I woke up there in the darkness. The darkness when it was beginning to be light, but it was summer then. In the night, in our house, it is very much winter now.

11

During the summer I longed passionately for winter to come. I imagined it every day. I saw snow falling into the dusty dried-out street.

And now it's come. 'Dark December's bareness everywhere'. I still prefer it; I don't imagine summer being here, or want it to be here. But in the deep night the winter does seem to be a part of our state, too much a part of it.

I try to evade sleeplessness by going up to bed late if there is anything any good on television – excitements, murders, shootings, chasing . . . After those I usually sleep quite well until Iris wakes me. After she is back in bed and all seems calm I find it difficult to go to sleep, and then begins my nocturnal compensation time, an hour or two devoted entirely to Belial's remedy, the thoughts that wander . . .

Although they are not exactly thoughts – more memories again, and, as it were, memory-creations. Much more satisfactory than dreams, even if the two have something in common. They are charms created or invented by the past, charms against the despair of the present.

If only there was some way of sharing such things with Iris. It doesn't seem so long since I used to talk to her about the things we had seen in Wales, when we had been there with Peter and Jim. The blue eyes of Cloudy their sheep dog, the pied flycatchers' nest beside the churchyard. I once reminisced to her about these things; and although she may not have remembered, it gave awareness something to do.

Now it has nothing to do, except to be aware of me. My smiles and jokes still reassure; but as it wears on they begin to be baffled by the sheer bulk of the day. How, at five o'clock of a winter's evening, to get through the three or four hours until her bedtime? Jokes wear thin; tea and biscuits she ignores; TV has become useless, even as another presence in the room, a distraction in the background.

I wonder: can even two- or three-year-old children, endlessly questing and chattering, be as exhausting as this vacancy? It fills my mind and heart too, paralyses the will, or whatever mechanism it is one uses to plan and overcome the next minute of being. No point in picking things up off the floor: Iris will have them back there in a few minutes. Or other things. Suppose I try to set up a routine? I undo what she does: she undoes what I do? But I haven't got the will for it.

'Please help me,' I say, smiling and trying to make something funny out of this appeal: and to my amazement Iris replies at once, 'Poor doggie!' And she has a smile too.

Thoughts or memories are only free when Iris is asleep. And in a guilty way they depend on disregarding her. They would hardly be free otherwise.

But was that always the case? The happiest marriages are full of alternative lives, lived in the head, unknown to the partner. Or perhaps not so unknown? Iris was leading such lives as she planned each of her novels, and I used to feel an obscure sense of participation. It was very satisfying. The fullness of her hidden life gave me as much daily pleasure as what we did together. In some way it felt as if we were more at one – just in my knowing that things were going on – than if we had been sharing them.

Iris would not have minded if I had asked about them – in fact she would have told me. But I never did ask and we both tacitly preferred it that way. A mutuality in business secrets. But now our daytime contact is so total and so overwhelming that night-thoughts can only be a way of escaping it. Day-thoughts too, when we are outside walking, as we did in the summer. With her hand or arm in mine I moved in a dream. All the convenience and all the vanity of day-dreams. Summer walks, and now winter night-time, are the place for them. And they cannot be shared.

That makes them proliferate all the more luxuriantly. And absurdly. Sometimes after a walk, or a sleepless night full of disturbance, satiety makes me feel quite bloated. Like a bird or an animal that eats and eats all it can, knowing that the winter is coming, or the ardours of the spring migration.

Once I was able not exactly to share a daydream with Iris but at least to involve her in it. There were occasions in the summer when she had escape impulses even on our walks, no doubt related to the wish to vanish out of the front door, to wander off somewhere, anywhere.

Nun weiter denn, nur weiter! Once she rushed abruptly up to a young man who happened to be passing. Tall, dark, obviously a foreigner. She caught hold of his sleeve. '*Help me, please, help me.*'

He looked bewildered. The urgency of the appeal not only bothered him but seemed to convince him. 'Please? What?' – addressing me as well, but at me he gave an accusing look. Was I harassing her? It must have looked like that, incongruous as it might seem, when the two parties were so elderly, and apparently so closely connected. Ah, but that was the trouble – the home was the worst place – the media would have taught him all about child abuse and granny-bashing . . .

I gave him a smile and started to drag Iris off by the elbow. Looking back I saw him standing still in doubt, and noted he was big and powerful, built like Bulldog Drummond, one of nature's rescuers and the hero of those stories by 'Sapper' I used to read in childhood.

So I started an instant fantasy along the lines of that Hitchcock film, *The Lady Vanishes*. As we reached home and I deadlocked the door on the inside I was already well into the scenario. Woman abducted in broad daylight. I, the kidnapper, a man of iron nerve, had easily persuaded the bystanders that I was in charge of the poor demented creature. On other occasions when Iris had demanded help from a passer-by I had tapped my head significantly to indicate that I was in charge of a deranged person, a gesture which usually embarrassed the parties concerned into making their own escape.

I got Iris indoors so precipitately that the back of my coat got caught yet again in the slamming door. It's becoming a habit. I had to undo the mortice lock and open the door to free myself, laying a restraining hand on Iris to prevent her blowing away like a plastic bag in the wind. Once off like that as she is difficult to catch. I marvel yet again – another of Dr A's almost daily repetitions, like the tail caught in the door – at the contradiction between her instinct to be away – anywhere anywhere out of our world – and her wish to be my shadow. My Water-Buffalo, interposing her bulk so that *I* can't vanish away.

I depend more and more on her dependence, and yet I also need to be exasperated by it. Nowadays I can deliver a volley of obscenities at her and she smiles and nuzzles me as if they constituted the deepest, most loving reassurance. 'Damn your eyes, blast your guts, bugger off can't you!' I shout it with a beaming smile, giving her a not too gentle push or a whack on the behind. Good for both of us, a real relief, and yet is it really so good for me? It's not like the violence she could feel once when she said, 'Don't hit me.' It's formalised, but something feral and fierce is lurking there none the less.

If that sounds portentous, what about that other glib stuff, beloved by romantics, about love and hate being close together? I don't believe that for a moment. Love is on easy terms with sudden rage, with violent exasperation, but surely not with hatred? Cold hatred? Or is that complacent?

When freeing myself with what used – how long ago it

[203]

seems – to be called filthy words, I sometimes push my head at Iris, saying, 'I hate you, you know! I REALLY FUCKING WELL HATE YOU!' To her it all seems to sound like a comment on the weather. The words fall down disarmed, but could they rise up in the night and mop and mow before her like malignant ghosts? 'He said that. *Did he really mean it?'*

But there is no memory involved – within seconds the waters of oblivion have washed it all away. A child says, 'I hate you I hate you,' and mother takes no notice. It is no more than a brief disowning of dependency. Iris now can be like a three-year-old, sometimes an impossible three-year-old. But it is I who say, 'I hate you,' and she, like the mother, who takes no notice. Just a happy look for a moment on her creased little face.

I think this happy look is because I am talking to her in a serious way, not just inattentively murmuring in reply to her gabble of unmeaning query. She catches the tone. More than that, which makes the relation of memory and understanding so strangely unpredictable, she still seems able at times to identify an old joke reference.

I used to quote the husband and wife from *Sense and Sensibility*. Young Mrs Palmer is an infinitely silly, infinitely good-natured girl who must have charmed dry clever Mr Palmer, an *homme sérieux*, into making her an offer of marriage. He puts up with the consequences however exasperating he finds his wife, who for her part is as delighted by his displays of bad temper as she is by everything else. 'Mr Palmer is so droll,' she tells friends with a fond giggle, after he has just snubbed her mercilessly in public. 'He is always out of humour.'

Mr Palmer is luckier than he knows. Or did Jane Austen perceive that he secretly loved his wife for her good temper, and because she enjoyed him most when he was at his most disobliging? However that may be I quoted the Palmers to Iris, implying that I was now in the habit of behaving as badly as Mr Palmer did. She understood me; at least her face split into smiles. The Palmers were still somehow there, lodged among the forsaken brain's disused and dusty files.

In actual fact Iris never much troubled herself about consulting those files. She never seemed to need a mental card index of her own, still less a computer. Creation with her was never in the least business-like, and I sometimes wondered how it got done at all. Could it, because so magical, vanish like the ending of a spell, as it did when the dark escort came for her? There was no struggle then, no protest, no fighting retreat. Her powers seemed to vanish between one day and the next. So many times previously she had told me, 'I've finished the novel, now it's only got to be written' – as if when the spell was in place the words would do its bidding obediently.

Her publisher marvelled at, but I think thoroughly appreciated, Iris's unworldliness and her indifference to business matters. All those things Norah Smallwood could take care of herself. Iris rather enjoyed being bossed about by Norah, who had the secret of doing it in a way that reassured and never irritated. For her Iris was like the clever little girl getting on with her own thing in a corner of the nursery, never expecting the attention of the grown-ups, still less their flattery and praise.

I don't think Norah, as effective managing director of Chatto and Windus, ever stood Iris a single meal in the course of their long and happy relationship, and never wasted an ounce of publicity on her.

Not that such practices were normal at that time, as they are with an important author today. When Aldous Huxley, then the most revered icon on Chatto's list, came over on a visit from California, Norah made the unusually handsome concession of inviting him for supper. But on the firm's premises, a supper she proposed to cook and serve herself. Iris and I were bidden, and told to report to Norah's flat in Vincent Square at seven sharp, bringing our car. There we heard we were to ferry the dinner to Chatto's cramped offices in King William IV Street, where I almost spilt a big bowl of salad when negotiating the narrow stairs.

Aldous Huxley, a man of sense and charm, seemed to regard this arrangement as an admirable one, and to enjoy it in the spirit of old Bloomsbury. But when Iris's New York publisher came over and wished to take her out things were very different. The gentleman from Viking Press regarded her almost as royalty, and took her ceremonially out to lunch at the Connaught Hotel, which is very expensive and where the oysters are out of this world, as my father used to say of Gerda's fish pie. Iris had no interest in oysters but appreciated the bread and butter pudding.

Her host, she told me, sat watching her devour this nursery dish with awed incredulity. But she sharply criticised the lack of drink, regretting the good strong martinis that Norah had served to an appreciative Aldous

Huxley and his fellow-guest Leonard Woolf. When I expressed astonishment that the gentleman from Viking had not plied her with booze, she admitted that he had taken a lot of trouble over a bottle of rare burgundy which was, she said, much too good for her. She would rather have drunk the house wine, and plenty of it.

Today, when Iris likes only a few drops of sweet sherry in her orangeade, and is more or less unconscious of it anyway, it seems hardly believable that she was once such a robust drinker, for whom a bottle of wine shared between two was, as she once put it in a phrase she must have picked up in Ireland, no more than 'the sniff of a cork'. She once told me that an old friend, George Lichtheim the political journalist, had taken her to task about this in an avuncular manner, alleging that he had seen many brilliant girls of her sort succumb to the demon drink.

I liked George Lichtheim, a temperate and benevolent man, who killed himself with a drug overdose when he developed cancer. That was many years ago. But I still mildly resent his presumption in advising Iris to go easy on the bottle, even though the advice was given long before I met her. Alcoholic excess in a misspent youth was not Iris's thing at all, however much trouble she may have had with what she had once termed 'the love business'.

Norah herself was no stranger to the love business: she had a close relationship with another director in the firm. Widowed in the war she was the soul of discretion about her authors with whom, in the words of Hilaire Belloc's satire on those who ruled the natives of some backward colony, she was always 'firm but kind'. This suited Iris's own modesty and inherent lack of self-importance. But once when Chatto's asked me to do a book on Tolstoy, and Norah raised some mild objection to the way I proposed to go about it, Iris sprang to my defence like a lioness watching over its cub.

On that occasion Norah backtracked hastily, in some surprise, for Iris was meekness itself when she sent in a novel, as if expecting that it might well be rejected. It was always in her own handwriting – Norah charging a stiff price for it to be typed – and I used to tease Iris by quoting some anonymous rhymester who had himself perhaps at one time experienced rejection by the firm.

> Take it like a trooper
> Your MS missed the bateau.
> Mr Windus thought it super
> But not so Mr Chatto.

It must have been many years since those half-legendary figures had been replaced by other directors, including the redoubtable Norah, but Iris always looked grave if I quoted this little rhyme. I think she really thought it might happen to her, as of course it did happen to poor Barbara Pym in the late '60s (ill-omened decade) when the firm who published her came under dynamic new management.

Pym's story had a happy ending I'm glad to say, and of course Norah received each new offering by Iris with cries of joy, although I suspect she did not read them much herself. Her own tastes were rather different. I once mentioned to her how much I had enjoyed *The Flight of the Heron* when I was at school. Her eyes lit up as she told me that D.K. Broster was a scandalously underrated author. 'So,' she said, 'are Margaret Irwin and Marjorie Bowen. I read *The Glen o'Weeping* every year.' She had once triumphed in the teeth of the Chatto board's more intellectual members by accepting a novel about King Harold by an American lady, Hope Muntz. It was called *The Golden Warrior*, and was in fact a rattling good yarn which sold quite well. I always thought of Norah as the Golden Warrior after that.

Before Norah died she went to the trouble of consigning Iris to the care of Ed Victor, a particular friend of hers and as it turned out the best as well as the most kindly of literary agents. Iris had never had an agent before, and though she had lost her mother publisher she now acquired a father figure who looked after her interests even more shrewdly and devotedly.

Ed rented a medieval cottage in the gardens of Sissinghurst, where he pressed us to stay sometimes in his absence. We used to feel very proprietary when the swarm of day visitors had departed and we had the gardens on a summer's evening to ourselves. Ed also flew over to shepherd Iris round New York when she gave a lecture there, and he showed her with pride the Brooklyn quayside where his father, a newly arrived Jewish immigrant, had once peddled fish.

Iris was not only good at friendship, being deeply interested in the lives of the people she liked, but she even used to extend this interest to professional interviewers, many of whom became 'pals for life' after merely expecting an hour or so of information-gathering for an article on the celebrated author.

I had cause to remember this when an American journalist who did medical articles asked to come for an interview. I made an effort to shepherd Iris into the drawing-room, where the children's programme we still sometimes watch was coming on, but she soon followed us into the kitchen and sat down in her own windsor chair.

Naturally we were talking about her, like two doctors discussing a patient, and the journalist looked a slightly anxious query at me. (She had already said: 'Don't answer any questions you would rather not.') I think I have followed Iris's own example, now that Alzheimer's has removed her from the ordinary decorum of daily life, in ceasing to feel any embarrassment about this sort of thing. The journalist's queries are euphemistic ('Do you have to help her on the loo?') but we both glance appealingly at Iris from time to time, as if for reassurance.

If that's what we are wanting we get it. Iris at least gives the impression of knowing exactly what we are talking about: her face has an expression of courteous but faintly amused interest. If the topic bores her she is too polite to show it – that's the impression – and the lady interviewing me soon looks reassured.

She is a nice woman, a doctor herself, and interested in the duration of the illness. More than four years now, I tell her. A question seems to be imminent – 'Do you still have – er – sexual relations?' I cannot help feeling curious to see when it will come. Feeling like a prostitute with a nervous client I give the lady a look of invitation, but Iris is now getting frankly bored and her air of polite amusement has disappeared. She jumps up, starts to mutter and tug at my coat, and the journalist never does get around to popping the question.

To be honest it wouldn't have been an entirely easy one to answer. It may seem straightforward enough – do you or don't you? – but sex can be vaguer than that, and just as felicitous. No act of the will, no 'What about tonight, darling?' Like many men of his generation the novelist Stendhal saw the Will as all-important. When young Julien in *Le Rouge et le Noir* is alone with Madame de Renal he counts the seconds to zero like a soldier about to go over the top, and then nerves himself to pounce. But the old indeterminacy in our own sexual relations seems to prolong itself naturally into the unending confusion of Iris's present days, in which those long periods of anxiety are followed by brief happinesses, inconclusive moments of peace and close embrace.

What I do have, though I wasn't going to tell the newspaper lady about it, is a fantasy sex-life that has become very much one of Dr A's friends, even boon companions. By proxy a friend of Iris's too.

My fantasies accommodate persons both real and imaginary, the real ones mostly from the past. Characters in novels are not exempt. Young master Holden Caulfield of *The Catcher in the Rye* used to dream about Eustacia Vye in Hardy's *The Return of the Native* – a piquant example of one fictional character having a fantasy about another in a different novel.

I still have a recurrent *tendresse* for one or two of Barbara Pym's female characters. Pym herself, much given to romance but not, it seems, to sex, observes that married couples have no idea of the importance of the *full* hot-water-bottle, an indispensable adjunct to the single bed in that unheated vicarage which features in many of her novels. That full hot-water-bottle could also stand as a kind of symbol for a lot of sexual fantasy during the last few distracted months, even though my own fantasies have been able to grow and blossom in the warmth of a double bed.

I seem to read hardly anything nowadays, but where was it I saw – some review or other – the comment about the murderer West and his wife, who chopped up young women in their cellar. *Lustmord*. They lacked the ability to imagine without enacting. Had they been producing *Macbeth* – an unlikely possibility admittedly – it would have meant nothing to them unless Duncan and Banquo, and Lady Macduff and her children, had really been butchered – and on the stage. For most of us the stage in the head is good enough – in fact what makes the head worth having.

Belial would have agreed, probably with a sly smile. I don't think he would have approved of the Wests' goings-on, devil though he was, but I'm sure he had plenty of sexual fantasies. Or perhaps not? He was in his own way a solitary spirit among that 'hellish crew' who seceded from God's love and abandoned heaven, and it may be that free and solitary spirits don't bother with that kind of thing. Their 'intellectual being' has other things to do. It is those who have become lonely in a relationship who find most release in fantasy.

I am not exactly lonely – how could I be when so close to Iris, every hour of the day and night? And yet that closeness without communication, however loving it may be, is also its own kind of loneliness. That's obvious. What's not so obvious is how much one comes to need both of them: closeness and loneliness alike. I know with certainty – but how? – that if Iris were to have to go from me, into a hospital or home, all these solitary and friendly pleasures, fantasies too, would vanish like a puff of smoke. I should not be lonely then, a happy state now with all Dr A's friends to keep me company. I should be abandoned.

With nothing in the head. I have no illusions about my ability to be a solitary free spirit. The solitariness of a close relationship – and how much closer could we get now? – is for me the fertile ground for fantasy, as it is for memories, the ones that go far far back. When Wordsworth wrote of the memories 'that leap/From hiding-places ten years deep', that was hardly a big deal. Any number of years deep. Sixty-five and more . . .

But such memories predate fantasy. A significant difference. When puberty begins the simplicities of memory disappear. From then on it is mixed with fantasy, almost becomes a part of it. After fourteen or fifteen, or whatever the age of puberty now is, memories must lack their primal truth. The earliest ones come back to me with the new force that is born of the present situation. Later ones have inherited in reverse all the fantasies that come to one's aid at the present time.

Fantasy and enactment are separate, and their co-habitation, to use a word slightly ridiculous in this context, is part of the charm of each. There suddenly comes into my head that absurd story, familiar to all of us in some form, of the sleepy wife murmuring, 'Oh do get on with it, George,' and the husband replying, 'Sorry, dear, I can't think of anyone at the moment.' Did Helen after the fall of Troy think of Paris when her husband Menelaus made love to her? No doubt she did but it's not quite the same thing. George was trying to think of someone he knew and fancied, a girl at the golf club perhaps. Someone he knew, or had seen from afar, but would never get anywhere with. That would be part of her charm, like that of most sex fantasy.

Did Jane Austen ever imagine being in bed with Darcy, or with Mr Knightley? It is possible, but seems unlikely somehow. Fantasy shrinks from the sharp edge of her intelligence, still more from her secret amusement at what people – herself included – might secretly be dreaming.

Such amusement is no enemy to love – on the contrary. If Anna Karenina had loved her husband she would have delighted in the size of his ears: the sight of them would have fed both love and amusement together. As it is, their all too familiar bigness only reminds her that she doesn't love him.

With fantasy the case is rather different. I am amused by my fantasies, but the fantasies are not, so to speak, amused by me or by the story they tell: they have to get on with it with the necessary concentration, as George would have done had he managed to 'think of someone'.

Love accepts the comic; just as it accepts what is merely sensible. 'An intelligent love'. One of the shrewdest critics of Jane Austen, sometime in the nineteenth century I think, coined that phrase for her own ideal. Was it the same man who quoted the Earl of Shaftesbury? Something about 'the natural free spirits of ingeniose men', who if compelled by circumstances into an imprisoning monotony 'Will find out new motions to relieve themselves in their constraint'. I do not regard myself as particularly 'ingeniose', and in any case Shaftesbury the philosopher and scientist probably had in mind something more intellectually ambitious than the imaginary pictures and possibilities that throng through my head. And the heads of most of us no doubt. But they are friends whom I have special reason to encourage.

One of the most sober and penetrating themes in Iris's novels, the later ones in particular, is the difference, where love is concerned, between fantasy and reality. It's true of course, and she pursues the truth in graphic and illuminating detail as only a great novelist can.

And yet I suspect that in practice the two creatures – love and fantasy – can love and live together in harmony without collision. Why not? You cannot fantasise about the being you love, that's true, and yet the being you love can inadvertently teach you things that will come in very handy on the fantasy side; where, as Shakespeare's Theseus puts it, 'the best in this kind are but shadows'.

Love, after all, can even teach you the ability to imagine without enacting.

Milton's Belial must have well understood this, and so incidentally did Shakespeare's Iago. Brilliant as is Shakespeare's portrait of Iago he has the difficulty of suggesting a man who is thoughtful and intelligent but also profoundly stupid; a man who, like those murderers the Wests, is ignorant of the difference between imagination and enactment. Wilfully ignorant one presumes, in Iago's case? For he knows that there are 'meditations lawful' in the human breast which never will and never wish to see the light of day.

There are thousands of potential Iagos, in offices and organisations, in military and political circles, who would dearly love to deceive and betray their bosses as Iago deceived Othello. But the wish remains at the level of fantasy, and probably not only does no harm but may even be beneficial to the psyche, something 'ingeniose' to relieve its constraint?

Much here must depend on the free play of consciousness, which means not only its intelligence but its modesty and humour. Iago was a witty man but not a humorous one. At bottom he was stupid as well as 'knowing'. And he had the mad self-confidence of the deeply conceited man. He should have been content with imagination, but the lure of enactment was too strong for him. It became a duty. A duty owed to the conviction of his own untouchable superiority.

Fortunately for us all, Thurber's Walter Mitty is a much more characteristic fantasist. His constrained homelife under the thumb of a repressive wife bestows on him all sorts of adventures in the world of the mind – lover, fighter pilot, cowboy, intrepid seaman. The film made from Thurber's original little sketch had the bright idea of mingling fantasy with reality. The dream girl, the damsel in distress, really *is* in trouble, pursued by genuine villains, enlisting Mitty's help to save her and the patriotic operation on which she is engaged. It worked because it was funny in the film. Humour came to the rescue, rather than Danny Kaye as real life hero. Fantasy always wants to be real, but never, I'm glad to say, succeeds. Intensities, whether in literature or in life, don't much care for humour.

And yet Dostoevsky – Iris too – are brilliant at combining comic and tragic in the complexities of a plot. In spite of Iris's theoretical warning she *does* mix fantasy with reality, but at the higher level so to speak.

I remember being amused once by an item in the agony column of a magazine, a superior fashion one which our friend the photographer Janet Stone used to read. A rather solemn young lady, a self-declared feminist, had written in some agitation (this was several years ago) to confide that she had the most dreadful daydreams of being seized, subdued and raped by a masterful lover.

What was she to do? – such things were entirely against her true female feelings, her wishes and principles.

A bored but kindly agony aunt replied: 'Don't worry, darling. We all have such desires deep down in us and they're quite harmless. Try laughing at them and carry on with the good work for women's lib!'

Sound advice, I'm sure, for those now old-fashioned times. And for our own. The modern spirit is too insistent on belief and thought kept whole and undivided. One faith, one conviction, one correctness. But surely Belial's 'intellectual being' does not work like that?

Who was it who described post-modernism as 'preemptive kitsch'? Not a bad definition. Kitsch is always in good faith: it honestly believes it is dealing with reality. Hence it can appear ludicrous to the latterday viewer, like King Arthur's knights and Victorian nudes. The artist has solemnly and unwittingly mingled fantasy with the reality of painting, or of words. Had he done it deliberately he would have created a new style of art. Like Roy Lichtenstein or Andy Warhol, who *knowingly* transformed the kitsch situation of a comic strip, or the fantasy world of an advertising label.

Knowingness is always total. It never accepts that we live by choice in different worlds. Two of them or more. And one of them at least always has a kind of innocence about it.

12

Musings and ramblings. Through them all I see Iris's face, looking both desolate and impish as it broadens into a smile. She is coming to me now with her arms out for the comfort of a hug, and because she sees I am smiling too. 'Aren't you a bad cat?' She has been banging the locked front door, making her histrionic moaning noise with an occasional 'Help help!' Sometimes a wild cry like an owl.

'Now don't be a bad cat. Be a good cat. Purr, purr.'

Iris seems recovered. So time to have a lie-down. It may be the journalist lady who has accidentally disturbed her. She consents to come to bed, a siesta, and I listen until her breathing is regular, a nice quiet noise that soon sends me off too. Or not quite off. A dream of fair women begins – how many there are these days! Not so fair actually. More fair-to-middling, as Samuel Beckett put it. But then I am asleep, and wake with a jerk. Something is wrong. No it's not. Iris is still beside me. Slipping away again I start to have a fantasy about a Gerrards Cross cocktail party, and a woman I meet there.

Has Iris been listening, just as I listen? She jumps up swiftly and silently and makes for the door. The lady vanishes. I know she can't escape but a siesta now is out of the question. No choice but to follow.

Iris is in the garden, by the padlocked gate. She has been shaking it and shouting; now she is shedding silent tears. She runs to me, buries her face against my body, clutches me as desperately as a three-year-old. As I comfort her I think of my dislike of babies and children, more than dislike – hatred – when I see them in the supermarket, showing off and screaming.

It makes me start to laugh, and Iris looks up at me, her eyes full of tears, and soon starts laughing too.

To know and see I can comfort her is still the greatest of my own comforts. But the impossible three-year-old will break out again at any moment. Best to go out. Walk therapy. That almost always helps, although Iris doesn't like it, and complains by shuffling along more and more slowly. I go on ahead and turn at intervals to make encouraging gestures. Iris responds and wambles a little more quickly in her endearing duck-like way.

Making quite good progress now. Round the Parks, and I notice with interest for the first time that the cricket pavilion in the middle is quite an elegant structure. Built around 1900. Only fourteen years to go before that innocent world came to an end . . . And what about old people with Alzheimer's then? Would they have been 'inside'? I suppose so.

Getting home is rather a struggle. Iris flags a bit but valiantly keeps going. At the front door she looks glowing, normal, neither her own age nor three years old but a healthy fifty say, a woman who enjoys walking in the country and has just come in from a good long hike.

'You enjoyed that, didn't you?'

She smiles beatifically. *'Oh I did!'*

An uncanny sense that all is well. Nothing the matter at all. How long will it last? When we are inside and turn away from the front door together I remember in the nick of time to go back and lock it.

So easy to forget this. To save the appearances I sometimes say to Iris that I have to do it because the Yale lock is broken, as well it might be from the way she shakes and bangs it. Iris looks politely interested and may even believe me; but I don't think she is concerned with the matter at all, or with drawing conclusions. How can she be? All she knows is that when the need to escape overcomes her she cannot get through the door.

The feeling of slightly insane happiness which comes over me at moments of success like these: when we have done something together and it has worked . . . ! But in fact we weren't exactly together. I led the way, like Hermes leading Eurydice back from the underworld, frequently stopping and turning back, as her husband Orpheus was not permitted to do. Orpheus lost her at the last moment by doing it, but I knew Iris would follow doggedly behind me, even if I had paid her no attention at all. I walked ahead to encourage her, and turned back to smile for the same reason. But she has not come from the underworld: she carries it with her, the dark place to which I have no entry.

Now all that is forgotten when we arrive at the front door, like a healthy country couple who have enjoyed their walk.

[221]

Enjoyed it, yes, but we weren't together on it; in the curious sense that we are when we stroll round the block together. Then we are together because apart: I am way off in my daydream, all about that Gerrards Cross cocktail party. While we are arm in arm, and Iris is talking in her own way, I replying in mine, nothing is easier than to vanish into a rapturous world of make-believe. It never existed before Dr A came along: now I could not do without it.

And so, this cocktail party, where was I? On that walk through the Parks I lost it entirely, or rather had no need of it, because we were really apart on our walk, and I had other things to do.

It was the Corbins who gave the party – real people. Friends of ours during the war. I was seventeen or eighteen then, but I can allow myself nowadays to be any age I choose – thirties, fifties, sixties, even my present seventy-three. But better at least a few years back?

Plenty of gin there seemed to be in the drinks of those days. I remember loving the sensation of swimmingness the cocktails induced. It didn't then in the least impair my powers of perception or locomotion, and it made me feel a lot less shy. So what might happen? Who might I meet?

Better make it 1953, the year I met Iris. Well, why not? I might not have met Iris that year: I might have met someone else. As with Poohbah, in *The Mikado*, that lends a touch of verisimilitude to an otherwise bald and unconvincing fantasy. For who is this someone else I meet at the Corbins' cocktail party?

The Perfect Woman of course. The woman who never

was, by sea or land. The idea of her is so wonderful, so comic, so grotesque, that I start laughing, and hug Iris's arm. As if obediently she starts laughing too.

'Evil into the mind of God and man may come and go.' Who says that? Is it Iago? Or someone in *Paradise Lost*? Not Belial I think. Perhaps it's Gabriel, the affable archangel? And why would he be saying a thing like that? Coleridge, I remember, lets fall somewhere in passing that moral evil can be explained by the associative processes of the mind. One thing leading to another . . .

Could my Perfect Woman lead me into adultery? I rather think not.

The idea seems so comic that I almost start laughing again. But the associative train is in motion now and I can do nothing to stop it. At least I don't do anything to stop it.

In my head I see the other people at the party, people I don't know. (Do they exist somewhere, and have I seen them without knowing it?) And the woman in the corner, my Perfect Woman, have I seen her before? Of course not, although there are hints and touches of resemblance: for example to the wife of some dignitary whom I once glimpsed at an Oxford lecture.

She stands in the corner, with an uncertain smile on her face. She wears thick-looking glasses. I want just to stand and look at her, but no one is talking to her at the moment, so social conditioning reminds me of my duty and impels me towards her. To her feet, as it were; for she is immensely tall, and as I approach I find myself gazing further and further up, as if at a lighthouse.

She is not only tall but big. Her huge hands are held

lightly clasped in front of her. Very clean they look, and white.

'What a nice party!' I say, gazing upwards, all my bright self. She looks down at me with her kind myopic eyes, as if I were almost too small to be visible.

'Yes, isn't it?' she says. 'Though I'm not really supposed to be here. A friend brought me. After church.'

'And do you live in Gerrards Cross?' (What a silly question, but she happily says yes.)

'So did we once. Not far from the church. Manor Lane.'

'Oh, I know Manor Lane.'

We beam at each other. The hubbub around us has grown more deafening. She leans down to hear what I next have to say, and I can hardly hear it myself. An ordinary woman fights her way through to where my Perfect Woman is standing, and I can just hear her say, 'We really ought to the going . . . in the oven . . . mustn't . . .' I see them smile at each other above my head. They move to the door, but the Perfect Woman turns and looks back at me for a moment with her kind unfocused gaze. Or is she looking at someone else? I shall never see her again.

Nearly home now, and lunchtime, which is never a good time. Iris usually fractious and depressed. She won't eat, but a good moment sometimes comes when I coax a spoonful into her mouth and she makes a happy cooing sound while her face returns to babyhood. I put another spoonful in, just to see it happen again. She is like a baby, but I hate babies. They repel me. And yet she seems herself again for some reason, her own self, when she accepts another spoonful and smiles up at me. Three years old.

And I have been smiling up at the Perfect Woman! The comedy of things! – it is almost too much to bear. Was I three years old myself when I first saw the Perfect Woman?

I don't meet the Perfect Woman again until the evening, when Iris is asleep and I turn out the light and get carefully into bed. Is she coming towards me now, taller than ever? No, the cocktail party is still going on, but has taken a different turn. No ordinary woman comes up to remind her about the roast in the oven. When the Perfect Woman left the party with her friend I knew I should never see her again. But here she is, and I am asking her about books.

Has she read *Georgina and Jane* by any chance?

'No, is it good?'

'I'm sure you'd enjoy it. I've got it in a paperback (were there paperbacks in 1953? Yes but not so many and various – only Penguins I think). May I lend it to you? I could send it. And do keep it. I've read it twice: I don't want it any more.'

Cunning little fellow that I am! The Perfect Woman falls for it. She looks a little bothered, but pleased too. 'If you could let me have the address?' Those great big hands are opening her bag.

'I've got a card somewhere. I use it for church work.' (Apologetically.) 'Here it is. If you really mean it?'

'Oh, I'd love to – I'm sure you'll enjoy it. *Georgina and Jane.*'

And it's done. The card is in my pocket now, like the key which locks our front door on the inside. And not a moment too soon, because the Corbin daughter is fighting her way through the party to me now, and saying Mother thinks we ought to be going. Something in the oven . . .

Memory here can give a solid back-up to fantasy. In 1953 there always was something in the oven on Sunday – the Sunday roast. Every household would gather round it for lunch. Mint sauce, roast potatoes. Queen's pudding to follow.

I eat the Corbin lunch, chat pleasantly I hope. The cocktail party continues to extend its animation over the family lunch table. We discuss hosts and guests. Someone says, 'Who was that great tall woman? Weren't you talking to her, John?'

I am thrilled by hearing her mentioned. So she really *was* tall? On the other hand it gives me acute pain that the others should have been aware of her, talked about her, however perfunctorily. She should have been there only for me. I can see her so clearly now, and I think of nothing else.

After tea I am taken to the station. Twenty minutes to the Oxford train. Corbin *père* has brought me in the Morris 10. A kind act, for petrol is still rationed. Politely I urge him not to stay, and fortunately he needs little urging.

As soon as he has driven off I leave the station at a fast walk. The card is still in my pocket and I have memorised the address. I remember the road perfectly from the time we lived here; I know just where to go. A substantial but modest house, Mock-Tudor front, plumy little conifers in the front garden; probably a bigger garden behind. I can scarcely believe in my own sense of excitement, and yet I long passionately to see this woman again, to gaze up at her glasses, her broad white tranquil face. But my pressing anxiety, tossed over and over in my mind as I hurry down the High Street and into Gaviot Way is, will she be in church?

She was there this morning. Would she attend Evensong? Quite likely, indeed almost certainly.

In which case she would not be at home. Would anyone else be? She had been asked to lunch by her friend who had something in the oven. That suggested she was unmarried, or at least not yet married. Or perhaps her husband was away? There are too many possibilities, and I try to stop them rattling pointlessly too and fro in my head. I must do something, take the bull by the horns.

But she wasn't a bull. It was Iris who had once been described by a mildly malicious friend as looking like a little bull. Coming towards you with its head lowered. Friendly, but formidable too.

I always remembered that description and felt great affection for it, although Iris had not been best pleased. She only liked to be teased by me.

The film stops. There I am, expectant. Full of an excitement I can hardly contain, and which has become almost painful. It would be a relief to break the whole thing off.

So I do. And actually I have no choice. It is just
beginning to grow light outside. Can the Perfect Woman
have kept me occupied all night? Time goes surprisingly
fast when one daydreams in bed, and I have probably
been dozing too.

I remember another thing from a magazine, *Woman's
Realm*, the one Iris's mother used to enjoy. Once it had a
letter from a young woman about to be married who was
asking the agony aunt if she would get any sleep at all
on her bridal night. The aunt advised her that it probably
wouldn't be as bad as all that; but she recommended
early hours and a hot milky drink at bedtime for some
days before the wedding . . .

Woman's Realm! Oh the innocence of those days, or at
least of those magazines.

What about a night with the Perfect Woman? But I am
uneasily conscious that Iris, who used to sleep so well in
the early morning, is already awake and stirring. A voice
comes, not drowsy but muffled. It might be Lazarus,
who after a week in the tomb has forgotten the use of
language.

'. . . Was a hemp . . . A hemphill, and when . . .'

Uncannily clear but muffled. Impossible not to listen
intently, to try to concentrate on what is being said, or
meant.

Suddenly Iris sits bolt upright. Old jerseys and towels
fall off her like the grave-clothes from Lazarus. With a
quick sure movement she is out of bed and out of the

[228]

room. The front door is locked, the key in my trouser-pocket beside the bed, but I can hear her moving through the house, as if on a systematic search.

Impossible now to turn the light on and read, impossible to stay in bed. What is she looking for? But I need not have worried. When I find her downstairs she looks like an old Russian woman come to market to sell old clothes. She has an orderly pile over her arm and is busily adding to it at every moment. I notice dishcloths in the pile, and a loose armchair cover, nearly worn through where the head would rest.

Poor darling. No rest for that head. And I need its agitations now. If there was peace and silence, if she were not here beside me, my fantasy about the Perfect Woman of Gerrards Cross, together with memories of Littlestone and the golf course and the Mixed Room and my ruined cottage – they would all vanish away together.

Like that puff of smoke. I've thought that before, many times, and it's true, even though I use it to cheer myself up.

At last Iris gets back into bed. Or half in, legs dangling. Her head and shoulders fall over on my side like a puppet's. I stroke her neck and hair. She gurgles happily a little; she is going back to sleep at last. Just when it's time for me to get up. At that moment there's a banging on the door. Mouthing obscenities to myself I descend as I am, see a friendly man with a big parcel through the glass of the front door. Half by signs I ask can't he leave it there? No, with an apologetic grin. Must have a signature. I go back upstairs, get the key out of my pocket, come back, open up and sign. The bulky object is for Iris. Probably six of her novels in Turkish. Or Hungarian. From the foreign publisher.

Trail back upstairs. Iris now beautifully, seraphically asleep, quite undisturbed. As she used to be in the mornings when I was able to sit typing beside her. She liked the noise she used to say when she woke, with a drowsy smile. But that was last year.

I shall stop calling her the Perfect Woman. Her perfection consists in not existing, which is what fantasy requires. And yet she's perfectly real for me. As are Mr Knightley and Mrs Bennet and the Pym heroines and all the rest of them.

Why don't I live in the real world? Does one ever? At the moment, in any case, I have excellent reasons for not doing so. Dr A and his friends all persuade me there is no such thing as the real world. They are good benevolent people, those friends of Dr A's, and well aware that I need all the distraction I can get from mere physiological reality. Escape is all.

I shall think of her as the Woman of Gerrards Cross. That is a more sober title; more, as they say, realistic. The Perfect Woman is a little too fanciful, even facetious. Shall I look at her now in a quite different way, prepare a documentary about her as an 'ordinary person'? Well, that would be quite a different sort of fantasy, like the documentaries and soaps they do on TV.

On our next walk that feeling of almost unbearable excitement returns. By reflex action I hug Iris's arm more firmly. I am in the front garden of the house at Gerrards Cross, between the plumy little conifers, wondering whether or not to ring the bell. No sign of life in the house.

I've done it! The bell sounds appallingly loud. Sensations of panic. Perhaps the door will fly open and I shall be staring into the face of that big barn owl, who once loomed away so soundlessly over my head. Perhaps she is no more than the memory of an owl?

Firm, rather loud footsteps. It must be somebody else. Wrong house? Too late to run away now.

She is even bigger than I remember. Enormous. And she does loom over me, standing in the doorway. Black shoes, such huge ones, her feet must be as big as her hands. Not flat shoes though; three-quarter heels do they call them? My eyes seem unable to travel further up her, not even to her stockings.

How did we get into her sitting-room? But there we are anyway. Fantasy is like the flight of the owl. Let's run it back, as I believe you can do on video – I've never been able to work ours. But I must get further up her than her shoes.

When my eyes finally managed the ascent I saw that she was smiling and that she did not seem surprised to see me. Her kind myopic eyes. I managed to say: 'I thought you would be in church.'

She is telling me that there was no Evening Service this Sunday. The vicar had to take Evensong at Chalfont St Giles. (Is that plausible? – probably not in 1953.) And by that time we are in the sitting-room and she is urging me to sit down. Nice shabby armchairs. Chintz covers. No smell of man.

But . . . I am realistic enough to know that there would then be an awkward pause. Awkward on my side at least, but I am grateful to see that she is smiling on unperturbed. How old is she? A quick calculation going through my mind. The convenience of daydreams means that they must be made inconvenient too. Forty-five? Forty-nine?

The separation now between Iris's world and my own. It did not seem there before the stage the disease has now reached. Even when she no longer spoke coherently she responded to what I was telling her and to all my emotional reactions. To clowning and teasing above all, and the pantomime of love that went with them. I might even have enacted the Woman of Gerrards Cross for her. But no – there would have been no such woman at that time: she has come into existence because of the separation.

The two worlds still co-exist easily enough, in a sound-less pathetic harmony. Even when Iris is silently scouring the house, or on the rampage downstairs, drumming on the front door and shouting to the outside world '*Help me – help!*' I have sat tautly in bed at such times, typewriter on knee, awaiting developments. Remembering Byron's lines, 'I don't much like describing someone mad for fear of seeming rather touched myself.'

But it isn't madness, and I can't think of it as such. It is her old familiar self, which means that I cannot remember the self that must once have been. This seems the only familiar one now, indeed the only one.

*   *   *

Reading some letters that Iris's biographer Peter Conradi has unearthed. Letters from Iris written during the war to a lover who became her fiancé. Gay charming letters full of fun and *joie de vivre*. But the hand, though bold and strong, seemed totally unfamiliar, and I could not recognise the person who was writing at all.

Strange. Because I feel I should also not recognise the Iris – my own Iris – of ten, twenty, thirty years ago. The Iris I know, and am so close to, is the one who is with me today.

After their student days Iris and her brief fiancé seem seldom to have met each other. The war kept them apart. They corresponded, a miniature novel in letters, but there is only one side of the correspondence. Iris did not keep his letters, except one, typewritten, saying he had met this other girl, and he was sure Iris would understand. Iris understood; and her next letter is as gay and as mildly teasing as ever.

The other girl was called Clare. She and her husband are both dead. But if it wasn't for Clare I should never have met Iris. Except as a famous writer she would never have existed for me at all.

And would she have become a famous writer? Virginia Woolf suggested that Shakespeare had a sister, equally a genius, who because she was a woman has never been heard of. Had Iris married her brief fiancé she would have stayed married. I feel fairly sure of that. She would have become yet another woman, one even more unrecognisable than the one whose letters I have been reading.

But what does that signify, as I shouldn't have known her?

*   *   *

How do I know, or think I know, that Iris would have stayed married? Just a hunch: but she is, or was, that sort of person. She would have had children too.

Would I have stayed married to the Woman of Gerrards Cross? But here, steady on, this is becoming absurd. There is, and was, no Woman of Gerrards Cross!

None the less I am sitting on her sofa. It is a dream within a dream, for I cannot get over my astonishment at having acted as I did. She seems less surprised than I am. Can she have fallen as instantly in love with me, in the few moments at that party, as I feel I have fallen in love with her? But come, come – even fantasy must draw the line somewhere. It works best if kept within bounds?

Why bother to try? Already the tape is shooting forward. Already we are chattering away on that sofa, my hand in her enormous hand (cool, soft). Already we are agreed that it had been love at first sight. And now to other matters. When are we going to get married, me and my big sane faultless woman?

Well, she will have to think about that. There are certain practical difficulties: difference in age and so forth.

'But nothing insuperable?'

'Oh no, nothing at all insuperable!'

Simultaneously we burst out laughing. But even in the joy of laughter we are melting slowly towards one another, as in old film romances, for the Kiss . . . At the last second we pause and take off each other's glasses, and start laughing again. And then . . .

13

When I was a tutor and Fellow of New College, already married to Iris, I had a few teaching hours with Dennis Potter, who later became the famous and innovative TV writer, creator of *The Singing Detective, Blackeyes*, several others. His reputation at one time stood very high, and I believe the BBC deferred to his lightest word. Potter was reading Philosophy, Politics and Economics, not Eng. Lit., but he asked to come to see me for some talks about authors in whom he was interested.

I liked Potter and got on well with him, but as a student he was a controversial figure in what was in those fairly distant days a conservative and stuffy college, not inclined to welcome or tolerate the defensively aggressive behaviour of this chippy young miner's son from the Forest of Dean. In such an atmosphere Potter longed for some sort of spectacular martyrdom. To be crucified with croquet hoops by sneering young bloods from some dining-club. Or expulsion by the college authorities for obscenity and irreverence, displays of which he hopefully provided. But the more he set out to provoke the gilded aristocrats, or to shock the academic bourgeoisie, the easier he made it for them to display their own sorts of encouraging patronage. His measure was taken, and the young Potter was often a frustrated and disappointed man.

His real moment of glory, however, and the exploit for which he was genuinely admired, was a production in the college cloisters of an early and obscure play of Pirandello, one which has been seldom or never performed either in its own country or abroad. I have forgotten its title, but Potter got his friends in the Languages faculty to produce some sort of translation, to which he added plenty of daring touches and bright ideas of his own. Even as an undergraduate in those dear dead days of the '50s Potter had the foresight to dedicate himself to the pursuit of the bad taste which was later to become the fashion; and Pirandello's youthful *jeu d'esprit*, which Potter had shown considerable enterprise in discovering, gave him plenty of opportunity.

In fact the play was harmless enough, almost quaintly so by modern standards. Potter played the lover of the young wife of a sea-captain, who fears her lover has made her pregnant. At the climax the wife, played by an upper-class student *ingénue*, beautifully unsuited to the part, agrees to put out flowerpots on her window-sill to inform her agitated lover in the street below that her husband, just returned from sea, is unsuspiciously performing his marital office. As the size and number of the flowerpots mounted the audience broke into rapturous applause.

Potter, his bright red locks flopping about and his flaky face glistening with sweat, kept glancing hopefully towards the college Warden, a venerable philosopher who loved to buttonhole reluctant students and show them round the ancestral beauties of the college. With touching naïveté Potter was clearly hoping that the Warden would rise in wrath and disgust and command the play to be stopped – he may even have hoped that he himself, as chief actor and producer, would be summarily cast out of the college.

If so he was to be disappointed. As the play went on, and the audience applauded, the Warden's austere features relaxed more and more into beaming smiles. When play and applause were over he strolled up to the crestfallen young man and congratulated him. 'A slight play perhaps,' twinkled the Warden, 'but a charming one, and your own resource and enterprise helped to give it body.'

Potter as a student had little to complain of. He met at Oxford people who would be useful to him later in his career, and he was able to try out some of the ideas he would afterwards make use of in his TV career. He did a lot of unusual reading too. Seeing in my room the Diaries of Francis Kilvert, the curate who lived at Clyro near Hay-on-Wye and recorded every day his meetings with his parishioners, his walks over the Welsh hills, and his own private feelings and longings, many of them surprisingly intimate, he asked if he might borrow them. At subsequent meetings we used to discuss Kilvert's daydreams, usually based on some harmless encounter with a young girl in a train, or on one of his walks.

Kilvert the Victorian recorded and wrote with a frank and lyrical innocence; there is nothing salacious about his diaries, although it was clear that they fascinated Potter in the same way that more openly sexual revelations might have done. Potter's TV fantasies, like *Blackeyes* or *The Singing Detective*, are in some sense a distortion or burlesque of the kind of material from which the parson Kilvert made his enchanting diary; but there remains in them too something of the same Victorian innocence. With a dollop of bad taste added of course.

When I first saw a bit of *The Singing Detective* on TV I found it so awful that I at once searched for another channel. Other people's fantasies not only discredit one's own but seem incomprehensible beside them. But I can see that Potter, in his own brilliantly exposed and as it were skinless fashion (almost literally, for the poor man suffered like the hero of his play from psoriasis), was the first to perceive how daydream can turn itself straight into TV script.

The old cinema dealt in public dreams, in some sense shared by everybody, and that gave them a kind of dignity, no matter how ridiculous they were. The Potter-type sex-dream is horribly intimate, and seems deliberately intended to embarrass us as individuals by an intimacy of bad taste. The critics who slated *Blackeyes* for its sickly brand of adolescent fantasy were being both self-righteous and hypocritical, for they could hardly have missed seeing that this was really the whole point and purpose of the charade.

I wonder if Potter, now among the shades where TV is no longer shown (I think he was dead before the age of sixty), might be amused by the daydreams of a septuagenarian who cannot quite decide what his own ideal fantasy age should be; but who firmly prefers, whatever it is, to indulge himself in daydreams not of young girls but of older women. Older, that is to say, than the ages he used to be. Now that I am seventy-three shall I start having daydreams about women of ninety? And so *ad infinitum*?

Well, never mind. It seems unlikely in any case that the Woman of Gerrards Cross would make a suitable fantasy for a Potter-type TV script. But of course I could be wrong.

Naturally I can discuss with the Woman of Gerrards Cross all the things I used once to talk about with Iris. We sit at the kitchen table holding hands and still gazing into each other's eyes (though we have now been married for some time) and we are eating something she has beautifully cooked – tender roast beef, a little underdone, with Yorkshire pudding, or boiled chicken with onions and bread sauce. Things it never occurs to me to eat at home and which in any case I wouldn't know how to cook.

Oh the vanity of daydreams! Their curious bashfulness can be comic too. I never do go to bed with the Woman of Gerrards Cross, even though later on we appear to have got married. As I hold Iris's elbow while she totters uncertainly round the corner of the block I contemplate the intensity with which I envisage this woman, seeing her eyes, her shoes, her big white hands, but nothing more intimate than that. I yearn for her none the less, a yearning whose dream existence has all the greater authenticity because it is never consummated in dream, as it so easily could be. The big Woman is, as it were, there for the taking, but I prefer not to take her.

Instead I stand with an arm round Iris as she rests against the lamp-post. Our short walk round the block is laborious now although she seems to wish to do it – I can't be certain even of that – and I am continually anxious that she may fall, that there won't be anyone about, that I shan't be able to raise her. This anxiety, real enough as it is, in no way diminishes the abstracted busyness with which my daydream is itself continuing.

How sure am I that the Woman of Gerrards Cross loved me at first sight, as I loved her? Oh, quite, quite sure. I see it in her smile. In the depths of her huge being she is secretly and joyfully incredulous that I should have fallen in love with her. But she knows I have. As she has with me . . .

The vanity of daydreams. And the pathos too. I fell in love long ago with Iris, and I was sure she had no awareness of me beyond a mild interest and liking. She fell in love with me much later, at a college dance. We scarcely danced at all.

Now she cannot tell me she loves me, and I cannot tell her that I do. At least not in so many words. The other day in the car she laid a hand on my knee and said with emphasis, '*Susten poujin drom love poujin? Poujin susten?*' I hastened to agree, and one word was clear. As soon as I could stop the car we kissed each other. She knew what she meant even when there is no meaning, and there was in that word . . .

Is my silent communion with the Woman of Gerrards Cross a daydream wish-fulfilment of what I know to be present, in this dreadful deformed state, between Iris and me? The desire to be loved. The desire to be shown that one is loved. In my daydream of the Woman I can feel it, and see it in her face and eyes. She does not have to speak of it, any more than Iris can do as we totter round the block together or drive in the car.

All the same the extent and refuge of my daydreaming has something embarrassing about it, even to me. But it has become part of this new way of life, and though it is so separate from it – hence the relief it brings – it is also closely connected. In the old days, before Iris was ill, daydreaming desire really would have been, and was, separate from our life together. But it was also far more fleeting, less tangible, less greedily to be relied upon.

In those days the agony aunt in the magazine could have given me the same advice that she gave the young feminist who had daydreams of being mastered and enslaved by brutal men. 'Don't worry, dear. It's quite a separate thing, you know.' Nowadays it is not so separate. It is much more pervasive, much more a part of my life, and one on which I am increasingly dependent. It is a true friend of Dr A, and of Iris too.

Communication difficulties. After an impossible night I turn on the light at five and start trying to write this. Iris is asleep. The sleeping draught did not work, but nature seems to have taken over at last. She lies peacefully, her face relaxed. But at half-past six she becomes restless again. The time just before was wonderful, like a pool of clear dark water, the sort of pool we used to dream of finding to swim in. She was asleep and I was tapping my typewriter. Total darkness in the sky outside; friendly darkness with no trace of dawn.

When Iris wakes the daily grind of non-communication begins in full force. But I have never known it as bad as this before. She sits on the edge of the bed, fiddling with the old dress she has picked up from somewhere, trying to put it on like a pair of trousers. I dread her in this position, which can go on for hours, paralysing my freedom of mind. I urge her imperiously and impotently to get back into bed. She does not ignore me, or pay no attention; she seems to be listening to a garbled message. On the Radio-Telephone in the army the operator would have been saying, 'I am not receiving you,' or 'Receiving you Strength One.'

I remember that from the wartime, from yesterday as it seems, as now I try to speak more clearly, more forcefully. It's as if Iris were a very foreign sort of foreigner, but with such a person one might successfully resort to pantomime, exaggerated gestures signifying bed – sleep. Closing eyes, putting a hand under one's head. Such gestures now would only alarm her?

As it is, the more emphatically I try to get over the verbal message the more worried she becomes. I want something from her – what can it be? She gets up, totters round the cluttered bedroom, comes back with a slipper, an old piece of chocolate in silver paper, bits of newspaper off the floor. She offers me these. Rejecting them I make a last appeal: 'Bed! – bed! – get into bed!' I try to have the face and voice of a doctor. It fails. Evidently sad and discouraged, Iris resumes her seat on the side of the bed, her shrunken legs looking so cold.

I know from experience it is useless to lift them up, tuck them in. She would resume her previous position like an obstinate plant, curling itself back to where it has to be. Coercion, however 'firm but kind', never works.

I sit propped upright on the other side of the bed, gazing gloomily at the typewriter. Still with my doctor's face and voice I find myself saying as clearly as I can (Strength Five), 'We're lost, we're lost.' I go on repeating this, forgetting the doctor and saying it more and more histrionically, self-pityingly . . .

Iris looks relieved and collectedly gets back into bed. So that was what I was wanting? Why didn't I say so?

In the wet summer of 1941 I used to walk every day down Hedgerley Lane, inhaling the complex smells of rotting sopping vegetation. Rose Bay Willowherb, drenched through and through, gave off a strange smell like nothing else. It was not exactly a nice smell, but I loved it. As I sniffed it up I used to repeat again and again my favourite lines from a poem by Edith Sitwell.

> The mauve summer rain
> Is falling again.

I wonder now whether the big Woman of Gerrards Cross (why does fantasy insist she should be so big?) ever walked down Hedgerley Lane and inhaled, as I used to do, the rainy scent of rotting willowherb. It would be a moderate walk from where she lived, if she ever existed.

And perhaps she did exist. I mean, I could imagine another kind of existence for her. She might exist not in a fantasy but in a novel. That would be quite a different kind of thing, more free, more capable of true development? If fantasy is developed it becomes not only more improbable, more subject to all the absurdities of wish-fulfilment, but more boring as well. Detail, which is the life of a good novel, may be equally convincing in one's personal fantasies, but has no proper neutrality. It is too much under personal control. Once again I remember Iris's comment, never spoken to me but coming in an essay she wrote, that fantasy and fiction are, and should be, two quite different things.

Essentially true, yes: for art, as it realises itself, must shrivel up the appeal of fantasy, turning its intimacy into openness. But art may begin in fantasy none the less. So what if I take the Woman of Gerrards Cross and turn her into a real person? A person in a true novel?

No. I would rather think of her walking down Hedgerley Lane and smelling the wet willowherb, as I used to do. In that strange scent I could keep her: she would belong only to me, never to any other reader . . .

There is a surreal sense in which Alzheimer's has turned Iris herself into art. She is my Iris no longer, but a person in the public domain. You could say she always was, and yet never so for me. Now even I feel that she has an existence entirely outside my own, conferred upon her by the Dark Lord who is drawing her further and further into his own underworld.

When she has to leave me to be in a home, a beautiful home no doubt, I shall visit her as a stranger. It will be like reading those letters to the man to whom she was briefly engaged, just after the war. I could not recognise the handwriting, or the young woman who had written them.

Those letters have disappeared, gone to Pieland as we used to say. What can have happened to them? Unlike the case of the pie, which remains genuinely mysterious, this is only a rhetorical question. Iris must have found the letters, not with intent or understanding, and left them somewhere else, perhaps dispersed apart, lying anonymous now amongst the innumerable debris of the house.

The same thing happened, comically enough, to my false teeth, and once to my glasses too. The glasses were soon found – Iris had put them carefully inside a vase, fortunately a transparent one; but the teeth were more elusive. The bottom set was under the bed, not tucked in very far. I found them by lying down and surveying the scene beneath there with a torch. It looked like the ocean floor round the wreck of the *Titanic*, littered with indeterminate objects coated with dust, like the ocean ooze.

I had seen the pictures on TV of the real *Titanic* lying unromantically amid her lumber, and buried in what looked like dust. As so often on TV, one look was enough. As the programme ground on I soon lost interest in it, and in the ship too.

But I had part of the teeth back. And before I wanted to eat the next meal I found the upper set too, left carefully by Iris in a little gap amongst the objects on the kitchen table. Those teeth have led a dangerous life, which is rather like saying that a regiment has survived heavy casualties. Twice before I lost that lower set when swimming and fish-watching. Replacements were necessary. Their comrades remain for ever in the sea's ooze, irrecoverable.

The letters are back. I found Iris wandering with them in her hand, together with a sheaf of other papers, bills, old colour supplements. She parted with them, and the bills and bank statements too, provided I let her keep the Sunday magazines. If I open them and turn the pages for her she closes them carefully, carrying them about like a talisman. Sometimes she sits for a few moments – she never sits for longer – and seems to study the cover picture. One has a particularly disagreeable-looking girl with prickling hair and a snarling expression, wearing a very short skirt of blood-red leather, her legs as far apart as the skirt will stretch.

A far cry to the Woman of Gerrards Cross. Why shouldn't the Woman of Gerrards Cross have come from Sidmouth, or Beaulieu, two places that have become much more recently familiar? Perhaps it's because I have never been back to Gerrards Cross? Fantasy prefers to find a local habitation in the remoter past.

Sidmouth we used to visit quite lately with Janet Stone, who had known the place as a girl and taken Reynolds Stone there when they were first married. The dear artist. Iris was so fond of him, and he returned her affection in his gentle absent-minded way, showing her fossils and telling her by the hour about Victorian printing-presses.

Reynolds was a versatile artist. He engraved on box-wood, painted magically sylvan watercolours, incised lettering on stone so beautifully that he was commissioned to commemorate Winston Churchill on a huge green marble slab set in the floor of Westminster Abbey. His sudden death in 1979 was a desolation for Janet, and a great grief for Iris too.

In the years before Janet died, and well after the time when Iris's Alzheimer's became noticeable, I would drive them for a brief holiday to Sidmouth, staying at a little hotel in a sort of crevasse that ran down to the promenade and the sea. The hotel was an old one and claimed some connection with the Duke of Wellington, which seemed unlikely. But the bar was stocked with an excellent Australian red wine called Long Tom, or maybe Long something else, of which we always drank a bottle at supper, and sometimes two. Although protesting that she must only have half a glass Janet loved red wine, and Long Tom disappeared without any difficulty.

I used to wonder if Jane Austen, reputed to have looked favourably on a young man visiting Sidmouth who never returned the next year to woo her, drank her glass of wine at our hotel. But that wine would certainly not have come from Botany Bay.

Hardy told a friend that when he imagined Tess of the D'Urbervilles he thought of a waitress seen for a few moments through the window of a Weymouth teashop. I had never seen the Woman of Gerrards Cross, I only imagined her; and when we stayed with our friends Diana Avebury and Bill and Lizzie Pease, beside the estuary near Beaulieu, there was no memory for me to keep of the yachting girls who glided past on the brown water down to the Solent.

To her craft on Beaulieu water
Clemency the General's daughter
Pulls across with even strokes.

Such Betjeman girls offered nothing to the imagination, even when they were sunbathing on some expensive vessel, whose sails, folding themselves as neatly as toy blinds in a doll's house, seemed merely for show. An invisible motor was doing the actual propelling, and Betjeman's Clemency would surely have scorned these modern mechanical aids?

In Diana's little marine flat I enjoyed watching some late night horror picture on television, when Iris and our hostess were fast asleep, and red and green lights were moving mysteriously outside on the dark water. I would turn the sitting-room lights off, and a ghostly masthead illumination outside the dark window made a backdrop for whatever Gothic goings-on were illuminating the screen. I sometimes turned off the sound so that the heroine's screams would not disturb the household.

At this silent moment of recollection there is a burst of swallowspeak in the bed beside me. Iris has woken up with the dawn. When we lived at Steeple Aston the swallows would wake us in summer, twittering away on the telephone wire outside our bedroom window. They would break off for a moment, and then one among the row of birds would think of something else to say, and the animated chatter would begin again, always ending abruptly with a word that sounded like 'Weatherby'. We called them the Weatherby family. Now when Iris bursts into a trill of meaningless conversation in the early morning, raising her head slightly and looking up at me, I reply, 'Hullo, Weatherby.' I don't think she knows now why I say this, but she always smiles as if she did.

I cannot *imagine* Iris. But then I never have done. She is not like the Big Woman of Gerrards Cross. Love does not need fantasy, nor imagination either, though I've never been clear what imagination means if it isn't my ordinary Belial activity, grown into a necessary habit now: I couldn't possibly do without it. To imagine women is so easy, and to me now is so necessary, but to imagine them is not to love them.

Shamelessness comes upon me now that Iris herself has gone, or is going. I don't care what I do write or say about her or about anything else. I know I am worshipping her no matter what I say. But these days I find myself proclaiming to others, and to myself as well: 'She seems to want to go to bed about seven,' or 'In this new phase she's very restless in the night.'

Who is this *She* who has made an appearance, and with whom others and myself are so familiar? We are familiar because we are seeing her from the outside. She has indeed become a She.

I feel that at moments with a shudder. It was a strange coincidence that those letters – letters written long ago to the friend who was for a short time her fiancé – should have seemed to be about a different person, and written by someone I had never met. The externalisation of Iris which has begun now, and which will inevitably continue and grow greater, is in a sense a more terrible version of that incredulity I felt when skimming through the letters. Whoever had written them was a She. Not Iris, my Iris.

My Iris is not yet a She, but inevitably she becomes more like one every day, even in my thoughts. 'When she has to go . . . What will it be like when she is gone? . . . What will I do when she is gone, into the home, the hospital?'

Did I write about Iris last year to stop her becoming such a She? It didn't feel like that, but the urge may have been there. And when it came out she loved to see the book, and the picture on the cover. She would once have never believed such a thing would be done, and have known that I couldn't do it, or have done it. Nor would I once. But it comforted me to see her smile in a pleased proprietary way, far away from it all as she now was.

I saw a glimmer of pride, almost of a fond and motherly pride, in the smile she turned on me. I had actually written a book about her! My brother Michael, who is so fond of her, approved the book too, and very warmly, though in his usual military manner. It helped the Alzheimer cause.

That was all the approval I needed, and disapproval there – from Michael or from Iris herself (and I know she would have expressed it somehow had she felt it) – would have been the only kind that I feared.

14

Belial thoughts also played once with a project that would have externalised Iris – at least to me, or for me – and for that reason it would never have been done or even attempted. But it remained a satanic idea, an idea not in the realm of fantasy but of true fiction. Quite a different thing. No friend of Iris, or of Dr A.

Novelists cannot but put 'real' people, or parts of real people, into their novels. Even Iris used to do that. She denied it, and it was true and right that she denied it, because she never did it with any revealing intention, or in any sense to 'portray' an actual person or a friend, no matter in what light. It was a generalised awareness of others that had entered deeply and powerfully into her imagination.

It was easy to see how far it had been transformed in the process, for friends sometimes ventured an opinion, never invited or welcomed, that person Y in a novel by Iris was based on person X in life. When such an opinion was uttered it was invariably wrong or misleading, because resemblances in Iris's novels were, so to speak, metaphysical, never personal.

She was amused once by something she had heard Evelyn Waugh say, and she told me about it, for Iris always appreciated an author who did not talk about his books seriously, no matter how seriously he may have felt about them. Waugh, it seems, had remarked that people never minded being put into a novel, provided the novelist commented somewhere in the text that the person concerned – the He or She – was 'good in bed'.

Iris also discussed this kind of question with a fellow novelist in a more thoughtful vein, at least on one occasion. That was Patrick White, whom we met in the '60s, on a tour of Australia organised by the British Council.

We both found White, with whom we had dinner one evening, a deeply impressive figure. There was something very strange about him, and quite unique, as if he had come from some lost civilisation which had existed long before the present settlement of Australia. He might have belonged to the Minoan or Mycenaean aristocracy, an impression somehow heightened by the dignified and hospitable Greek with whom he lived in a house near Sydney. As usual Iris asked him about himself in a way that never caused offence, and which completely overcame the withdrawn and slightly forbidding manner – very un-Australian – with which he began the evening. They talked about each other's books, and I was surprised by the way in which Iris, who normally never mentioned her own novels, became as forthcoming on the subject as White himself.

They agreed that the great novelists – both admired and cited Henry James and Dostoevsky: both implied a lack of fondness for E.M. Forster and Virginia Woolf – never struck them as making use of the novel form to give their own theories and their own egos an airing. As White put it, they never 'made use of the helpless individual'.

This somewhat Delphic observation appeared to strike an immediate chord in Iris and their discussion grew animated. Art, suggested White, is the very opposite of the capitalist instinct: true art never exploits. Although he admired D.H. Lawrence's writing he deplored the way in which Lawrence, while expressing a lofty contempt for the human ego in art, set up a kind of Punch and Judy show in his novels and stories, in which his own ego could maintain an effortless superiority over the personalities of his friends and the people he met, all of whom were made use of to display their weaknesses and deride their sense of themselves.

White asked if we knew the Australian artist Sydney Nolan, who was then living in England and whom we had once met with Reynolds and Janet Stone. He and White seemed totally different and yet they had something in common – a touch of strangeness. In my memory of that time the pair associate, as wandering memories will do, with our clandestine swim in the Swan river at Perth, and with the flight of black cockatoos in the outback behind the town.

Sydney Nolan's face had lit up when I mentioned those cockatoos to him, and he looked oddly haunted, as if that spectral avian crew, whom I had once seen clamouring through the dead timber, had reminded him of a need to return home.

Dear Reynolds Stone loved birds too, but his own watercolours, painted in the wood behind the Rectory

JOHN BAYLEY

at Litton Cheney where the Stones lived, could hardly have been more different from Nolan's pictures.

When lying beside a sleeping Iris I greedily let these memories slide on, coalesce, drift apart again. Her sleep is doubly precious now, relieving her of the sightless and timeless troubles which perplex her day, troubles of which those dark birds, winging out of the past, can appear in my mind like ominous harbingers. All such memories release me none the less: release me into that inevitably selfish world of sights and sounds I can no longer share with her.

I shudder now when I think of the place where Iris briefly became a *She* in my imagination. It was probably mere coincidence that it should have happened where it did, although things had been getting steadily worse, and particularly if we had to do a long drive. As the miles go on Iris becomes more and more agitated and restless, clamouring beside me in the car like a demented cockatoo. Stopping at intervals does not help, and I have learnt never to undertake such journeys, on whatever pretext. Our car had no childproof locks, and I used to be terrified that at the height of one of these manic fits she would get the door open and jump out into the road.

But there was no escaping such a journey on this occasion. Janet Stone had died at last. During her slow decline we had become much attached, and we tried to see her as often as we could. She was concerned about Iris, giving her the materials for embroidery and trying to teach her the simpler methods, though it was no use.

Janet herself had never got over Reynolds Stone's

[254]

sudden death. She had tried to make a new life for herself in her Salisbury cottage, devoted like a museum to her husband's paintings and engravings, but she missed him and their life together too much for recovery.

The nightmare drive had worn me out and made it impossible to think about the funeral, at which I had been asked by Janet's children to 'say a few words'. Never an easy assignment, this was likely to be an impossible one in present circumstances. Oppressed by our own troubles I could think of nothing to say. Perhaps something would come to me at the last moment, in the church at Litton Cheney?

Beside me in the car Iris babbled and gestured unceasingly, anxieties rising to a pitch in a weird shrill cry I had never heard before. A word or two came through. *'Wrong! Driving! Not way! Not mother, not house . . . mother house!'*

I called on all the friends of Dr A to help me, but for the moment they could do nothing. No desires to conjure up, no fantasy to aid, no memories . . .

Only one friend, and he a terribly dubious one, had the idea of doing something for me: and that was not until we were on the road home. With Iris in this state home itself was not a refuge of promise. Not a 'mother house' as she had so strangely put it. The madness would be there back home to meet us. As death had met the Eastern merchant in Samarra.

At last we were through Dorchester. On the bypass my own agitated gaze had flickered between the road ahead and Iris's hands – none too clean as usual, that was my fault – scrabbling near the door-handle. If only we could have come to the funeral by train. But Oxford to Dorchester by British Rail had seemed an impossible journey, and Iris could be as bad on bus or train as in the car, to the consternation of her fellow-passengers.

In the biography he wrote of himself, and pretended was written by his second wife, Hardy told the story of an American visitor who asked him what was the finest view in Dorset. After some hesitation he opted for the high road above the village of Litton Cheney. The sweep of Lyme Bay below, Portland on the left to be seen on a clear day; to the right Golden Cap and the capes beyond Lyme Regis.

Above the Bride valley the monument to that other Hardy, a distant relation, who had sailed the *Victory* past Portland on her Admiral's last voyage. It looks rather like an old-fashioned telephone receiver, upside down.

A deep relief to turn off the main road at last and dip down the lane towards the village. A sea fog was rolling up over the churchyard. The first snowdrops were showing among the turf on Reynold's grave, with Janet's newly dug and ready beside it. I thought of Reynolds's endearing way of talking to Iris; talking as if to himself, but with his bright eye fixed on hers, its affectionate gaze seeming to make speech unnecessary.

He used to read the Lessons in church. I never heard him, but I wondered how he could have done it, for his voice never rose much above a low murmur, breaking through one's own voice if one had begun speaking, like the sound of the sea. Nobody ever minded being interrupted in this way by Reynolds.

I silently invoked his aid as we walked past the grave

to the west door of the church. He loved taking Iris to the sea, on the long sweep of the Chesil Bank below us. He helped her to find stones. In summer the three of us bathed together, and once Iris nearly drowned, with us two men standing placidly chatting together as we dried ourselves. There was always a slow surge on the steep bank of shingle, but it was easy to judge the moment and let the sea bring one up. Iris had happened to misjudge it, and had been pulled under by the slight undertow. She had not panicked and the next wave brought her in. Reynolds and I, calmly chatting, had noticed nothing, nor did she say anything to us, although she told me what had happened in bed that night. She had used her memory of the moment in one of her novels.

We walked slowly to the church door, Iris fretting sadly beside me, supported on her other side by little Emma Stone, now a mother with three children. Her husband, a wonderful illustrator of children's books, had designed the jackets for my own novels. I had hoped originally that he would do the jacket for Iris's next novel, but the next one never came.

Janet never had flowers inside the Old Rectory, and hardly any in the garden – Reynolds preferred green leaves and bushes and trees. But the church was full of the pure cold scent of snowdrops, for which Janet was prepared to make an exception. Her two daughters had laboriously picked them that morning in the garden of the Old Rectory, with the permission of its new owner. They were massed in jars round the altar and the pulpit.

The sea fog had cleared now, and through the west

window I could make out the line of the bay. Could I get by if I were just to give a little commentary on these things, like a radio reporter at a sports event? Sea and snowdrops, and some past events? Placid chats in the hot sun on the Chesil Bank, near drownings . . . ?

I gazed for inspiration at Iris, sitting between the Stone girls in the front row. She looked like a prisoner under escort and was staring down at the marble floor. It was thick with worn old inscriptions, records of parsons and gentry long departed.

My eye followed her gaze in a bemused way. What *was* I to say when the moment came? And it was just coming . . .

I got out of the pew at the right time and took position on the chancel steps. I opened my mouth. Would I be able to get anything out? The small congregation looked expectant, but also, I thought, a little nervous. They were playing their part, as I would have to be acting mine.

Only Iris, lost now in her own darkness, seemed to have no role to play. There came into my head a line from Auden, from one of his plays. He remarks on the difference 'between the sane who know they are acting and the mad who do not'. Does Iris know the difference? I'm sure she doesn't as she sits there, gazing uncalmly at the floor.

I was able to speak at last thank goodness. I found myself saying that I missed Janet very much. Because I liked to tell her about funny things that had happened. Things, I was about to go on, which I could no longer tell to Iris, but I stopped myself just in time.

Unnerved by this narrow escape I found I had completely dried up. What else was there to say? I must give an example. Things that Janet had liked hearing about. Mind was a blank, but the mourners in front of me were still nobly acting their part and I must go on playing mine. Starting with a jerk I found to my horror that I was telling them the story about Audi and the bath.

Audi Villers, our old friend, now a widow, who lives in a quiet village in the centre of the very unquiet island of Lanzarote, had been staying with us recently. Just for the night. She had to go back next day to see an opera in London.

Soon after she had arrived I found her cleaning the bath. 'Audi,' I said, 'please don't bother. There's no need.'

Audi looked surprised by my words, and also amused. 'Oh yes there is,' she said. 'I want to take a bath.'

Sound logic. But why should it have struck me at the time as so funny? Anyway it did, and we had both burst out laughing. The congregation could hardly do that, but they also looked bewildered. What had this domestic event to do with their departed friend Janet?

To me it was clear as daylight, but to them, naturally enough, it was not. I hastened to explain that since Janet had loved comic things and happenings I was looking forward to telling her this one. Now, alas, I should not be able to . . .

It was too late for my realisation that the funeral audience had not found the story of Audi and the bath comic at all. Perhaps it wasn't? I had to hasten on, but how? Uncertainly I got out once more how sorry I was that I never saw Janet again, and so was unable to tell her the story. Some faces – those of Emma Stone and

Phillida her elder sister – did look touched and tearful when I said that.

Greatly encouraged I had, as I thought, a sudden brainwave, a recollection of the moment towards the end of Tolstoy's *Anna Karenina* when the heroine, on her way to the station to throw herself under a train, sees a shop sign that strikes her as comical. She thinks she will tell her lover Vronsky about it – it will be something to amuse him. Then she remembers she will not be seeing Vronsky again – not ever.

Tolstoy implies that if anything could have deterred Anna from suicide it would have been the realisation of that moment: the joke, the pleasure of telling it to the man she loves, the awareness that their love is over, and that life will soon be over too.

With the madness of those whom the gods wish to destroy I babbled out all this. How very apt it was, and how wonderful and touching was Tolstoy's art! By the time I ran out of steam the audience was looking not only bemused but downright uncomfortable. I still go hot and cold when I think of that moment. How could I have supposed that Anna's suicide would be a suitable topic for 'a few words' at a friend's funeral?

The business was over at last and we were on our way home. Even before we started Iris had become difficult. The kind Stone daughters did their best to soothe her, but her behaviour, normally so subdued in public and smiling, as if she were anxious to show that an Alzheimer sufferer could none the less play the part sweetly, became rude and wild. Like a bad child she wanted to go; and amongst the decorum of the funeral gathering, the sherry glasses and the teacups, she made her wish all too clear.

As I got her away, feeling by that time fairly wild myself, I reflected on the fallacy in Auden's smart epigram. It is the mad, not the sane, who behave as if they knew they were acting, but their parts get mixed up. However strange – 'naturally' strange as it were – Iris may have become in private, carrying odd things about and babbling away to herself downstairs at two in the morning, she had managed to preserve up to now the public part of a deranged person doing her best to conceal and apologise for what was wrong.

The funeral, I saw, had seriously upset her. Over-excited her too. That was why she had become the impossible child, seeming to throw herself with diabolical energy into the part.

Loneliness, as I drove and tried to quieten Iris, seemed overwhelming. I felt I longed for death, like Anna Karenina abandoned as she thought – no, as she knew – by a lover who had become a stranger to her. The person beside me seemed a stranger too. And I should never tell the joke about the bath to Janet Stone who was dead, and who I felt at that moment might have saved me.

All Iris's friends were far away. At the funeral the congregation had the look on their faces of those embarrassed by a mad person. I must have been mad to say what I had. Even now the Stone family must be regretting together their misguided wish that I should 'say a few words'.

The mourners had looked up at me with incomprehension and embarrassment. And Iris had looked down at the floor, with its marble records all worn away. No joke to be shared. I had never felt more hopelessly out of touch with her than at that moment.

Then I saw the house.

The little villages hereabouts were built of grey stone from Portland, nestling in their valleys as naturally as sheep in a field. This house was unexpected and nightmarish. It stood on a hill, proclaiming itself, built in the Olde Worlde redbrick style of the '30s. A long avenue lined with little conifers led up to it from the main road, and where the avenue began a fancy oaken gate stood open.

It was an odious house. And at once, as if despair and loneliness had brought them, things which seem to come from it and to be about it began to crowd into my mind. At that moment, with Iris raving and fretting beside me, the Belial in my head would have greedily welcomed any guest, no matter from where.

What came was like a dream, but it was also a story, a fiction, and it was hateful. My need for it at that moment was hateful too. This was not memory or fantasy, Dr A's faithful and comfortable old friends. This absurd nightmare which I started to tell myself was like a revenge, engendered by the demons of solitude, a revenge taken on the mad stranger screaming and protesting beside me.

In the car we had passed by the gate at the bottom of the avenue. But in my mind we had driven up that avenue. The woman beside me was indeed my wife, whose name now was Priscilla. She was a tiresome girl with whom I was on bad terms. I had a job in London with which I was as dissatisfied as I was with my wife, and my prospects generally.

Priscilla is hissing something at me. 'Why on earth did you do that? You can't just drive up to a private house.' I don't know myself why I did it. Something made me turn off the road, drive up the avenue. Why I don't know.

I ignore the hissing of Priscilla because I have seen something in the mirror. A man has stepped out on to the drive behind us. He has a scythe over his shoulder, and as I watch him he puts this scythe down across the avenue, as if to prevent our turning back.

I stop the car and Priscilla at once jumps out. She shimmies up to the strange man, all apology and London charm. She talks to him, smiles at him. He has a massive face and head, thick black hair. He is squat and sinister.

Where have I seen that man? I know him, I'm sure of it.

Of course! He is Dr Elias Canetti, the distinguished author, Nobel Prizewinner. Why should he be here, of all people? No wonder Priscilla seems to be so taken with him. He is a truly fascinating man.

In the time before Iris and I were married – how long ago it seems! – I was terrified he would carry her off, like Pluto into his own dark underworld. But Iris escaped in time, fortunately for me.

And here he was, back again, growing out of my head in the story I was beginning to make up of the nightmare journey.

I get slowly out of the car. I join my apologies with Priscilla's. Canetti smiles. His smile is that of a crocodile.

We have been invited into the house. Inside the house, sitting vaguely behind a tea-table in the drawing-room, is such a nice-looking woman. Tall, willowy, angular, faded, middle-aged. But so sweet-looking. I feel drawn to her immediately.

If only I could leave Priscilla with Canetti and go off with this woman! Away and away! I turn politely towards the host, the massive squat saturnine man, who bows and smiles his crocodile smile at me. He knows what I would like to do.

And he wishes me to do it. He always gets what he wants. He is the primal power figure. Iris's one-time lover, tyrant, dominator and master. Teacher too, and inspiration. The great all-knowing *Dichter*.

And now he will take Priscilla, whoever she may be, and give Iris to me. The sweet-looking woman sitting vaguely on the sofa.

Why is he doing that? Of course I know why he is doing it. Because his wife, Iris, who has for so long been his captive, has now for that reason begun to go mad . . .

But he will not tell me that of course. I shall learn of it too late. And Iris will then be taken into the other Dark Lord's domain.

Has Iris really belonged to Dr Canetti, all these years we have been married? Just as she has belonged for the last four years to that other doctor – Dr Alzheimer?

*   *   *

The car swerves violently. Iris has pulled at the wheel as I sat beside her driving, lost in this nightmare.

WE MUST STOP! Anywhere. Anywhere. During my dream, no fantasy but a loathsome scenario for a revenge novel, a hateful novel, we have passed Salisbury. And Hungerford too?

No we haven't – what am I saying? – I have been so lost in that dreadful story. I will not think of it as a fantasy, one of my own. It seemed imposed upon me from outside. An alien threat, as Canetti himself had once been. When I first fell in love with Iris she told me of this strange and wonderful man, with whom she had been and still was in love. When he learned about my existence from some third party he forbade her to see me. Fortunately she ignored that. But the shadow of Canetti seemed in those early days to stretch all the way from Hampstead to Oxford.

Canetti died in Switzerland a few years ago. He was married again, with a young daughter. Year by year he had grown more famous throughout the German-speaking world, until the eventual award of the Nobel Prize. He must then have been over eighty. He and Iris were always on good terms. She advised him about his daughter's education. But they had not met for a long time, more than a generation. I had quite got over my early fear and horror of the great man, a childish fear, as if he were a devouring ogre; and I believe that in some sense he could indeed be that too.

I had enjoyed his books. One about the Jewish community in Morocco I had especially admired, and he was cordial on the rare occasions when we had met. 'I like you,' he once said, confronting me in an amused way with his giant face and squat body. I blushed like a girl and escaped as quickly as I could, for it seemed like a dismissal. Not an unkind one but it made further communication impossible. Canetti was good at doing that.

And here he was, reappearing from the past, in an ugly house on a Dorset hillside. As he had once said, 'I like you,' he said now, 'I give you.' I am giving you this madness, this mad woman . . . To have and to hold, to love and to cherish . . .

Dr A's friends would shake their heads. And I must be going dotty myself, what with the funeral, and the sympathetic eyes, and getting it all wrong like that. And who was this Priscilla anyway, whom the house on the hill had dragged into its story? An awful girl she was – I could still see her quite vividly – and Canetti was welcome to her.

Humour, normality, love. Quite suddenly they seem to come flooding back from beside me, for Iris has gone quiet and I can feel her relax. I reach out a hand and hers finds it and holds it. Instead of stopping the car I feel we can now drive on tranquilly, for we must be on that lonely stretch of high Roman road that runs between Collingbourne Ducis and Wexcombe. A beautiful stretch in summer, when we always have stopped on our drives north and south to wander about for a few moments, contemplate the lofty upland, the clouds over Inkpen, and sometimes the insect dots hovering there which are hang-gliders, soaring and sailing among the huge curves that run down to the plain – the Great Plain as Hardy called it.

Good memories come back again now, like the good warmth that is flowing from hand to hand. In spite of the cold drizzle falling outside.

I remember when we once had the idea of crossing the Great Plain directly. A faint dotted line, I had seen, was marked on the map, leading from the deserted village where the country road comes to an end. All beyond has become an artillery range. I pointed out to Iris that the only truly unspoilt bits left in England are where the army has taken over, and sits growling like a dog in a manger. Growling far off maybe, but scarcely ever present or visible. I reassured Iris that the gunners were never there, and if they should happen to be they were compelled by law to give ample warning of their presence.

And we managed it somehow. The summer was an exceptionally fine one; we spun along over the smooth dry grass. At one point a milestone was embedded in the turf, with elegant incised lettering, probably from the 18th century, which showed the miles to Salisbury. We were on the old high road from London and the north, which once ran direct across the plain.

Iris had the naughty wish to take that milestone home with us. She always felt all stones belonged to her. But fortunately it proved too deeply embedded in the turf.

I wondered then if the deserted village was the one where Anna was born, the girl in Hardy's story 'On the Western Circuit'. So remote is the village that there is no school and she has never learned to read or write. She becomes a maid in the house of a wine-merchant's wife in Salisbury, where a young barrister working on the Western Circuit sees her riding on the merry-go-round at the town fair. They fall in love, and when she finds she is pregnant she begs her mistress to write letters for her to the young man.

Childless, neglected and lonely as she is, the wine-merchant's wife falls in with the idea, and presently she is herself in love with the young man, by courtesy of the postal service. The young barrister is so charmed by what he thinks are Anna's letters that he determines to marry her, and at the wedding the truth comes out. It is the only moment the real lovers meet, but the barrister finds himself 'chained for life', says Hardy all too predictably, to the wrong woman, an illiterate village girl.

Thinking now of Anna Karenina's last joke, never uttered; and of that other poor Anna, trudging across the wide plain to Salisbury and to her destiny, I remember also the woman I once knew whose husband had Alzheimer's. 'Like being chained to a corpse you know,' she had remarked to me with a cheerful laugh. I saw what she meant, for Iris's own affliction was just beginning to become severe, but no – it was not true. Not true for me then. Or for Iris.

And thinking this now I stop the car at last and put my arms round her. A few miles back I had felt for the first time since we met, nearly fifty years ago, afraid to be alone with her. I had found myself alone with a mad woman. One quite alien and strange, as the Canetti story I had found myself telling myself had suggested.

All that was gone now. She was just Iris, Iris as I had always known her, and loved her.

It was true we were in darkness, but it was a darkness without fear or hope, a darkness in which we were travelling now together again as one. And we could go on together somehow, from day to day, from tea to supper and from supper to bed-time. So long as we went on like that there would be nothing to care about, only the care that was between us. In giving it I received it back, twice blessed.

For by needing me now Iris also sheltered me, nourished me simply by having nothing to give of which she could be conscious. In losing her own, Iris had given me a new life. How could I live without her now, and without her friends, the friends of Dr A?

'Hear what comfortable words . . .' The Bible says that somewhere, or the prayer-book. And it's true. But comfort must have its end, as fear and misery do. Nothing is less predictable than dementia's ups and downs.

And as if to prove the point Iris suddenly wrenches the door open and plunges out, to vanish without a sound into the darkness.

It is so unexpected that for a moment I cannot even stop the car. I saw some miles back that she had got her seatbelt off, as she almost always does. She hates its constriction. And I had not the heart or the will nor the courage either – for that was at the time she was so far away from me, and I myself so lost in that vile Canetti nightmare – to stop the car and to put the seatbelt on again.

We were rounding a corner, going uphill, and I needed both hands on the wheel. There were headlights behind us too, following us up the hill. I had to brake to a stop on a corner and the car behind rushed past, missing us by inches and sounding a furious horn.

Inane thoughts went through my head as I scrabbled at the door-handle to get out, just as Iris had done. We had been to a funeral and done badly – badly then, and now, and in between – in all sorts of ways. And one funeral could so easily lead to another . . . to a couple more at least . . .

The road was quiet now, quiet as the grave, and so dark that I could see nothing beyond the lights of the car.

'Puss! Puss! My old mouse, my old catmouse! Where are you?'

No sound or reply. A strong cold wind was blowing steadily over the empty down. In the daytime here we had seen the racehorses at exercise, cantering across the downland in long cavalcades.

I groped my way back on the slope, along the side of the road. I shouted again and again. My voice sounded muffled and distracted, and the wind blew it away. The place seemed quite empty.

Has the Dark Lord appeared out of the earth and carried her down with him to his kingdom? Or did she herself deliberately invoke the help of Dr Alzheimer's last and best friend?

Blind terror now as I rushed further and further down the road. How far back could it have been? Another car's headlights approaching, shooting swiftly towards me up the hill, and I peered down the tunnel of light, half hoping half dreading to see Iris standing vacantly in the glare of it, silhouetted against the headlights of the onrushing car. Then I was crouched against the hedge as it tore past me.

And all I thought was: I have lost my Muse. I can do nothing without her. Without her I shall have nothing to write, and nothing to do. Instead of searching for Iris I crouched against the hedge and thought about that sort of thing.

I tried to pull myself together a bit. She must be here somewhere, like all those things that get lost in the house. But many of them are never seen again.

Suddenly there was a sort of noise coming to me in the wind. Not a distress noise, not a cry for help. It was more a sort of chuckling sound, faint but not far away.

Down the road again a few further steps and the shadow of the hedge lifted: there was a long gap in it. I plunged through and immediately lost my footing. I found myself rolling down a steep grassy slope. As I picked myself up, breathless, I found Iris was beside me. She was lying on her back and laughing, quite unhurt. After jumping out of the car she must have fallen down the slope, just as I had done, and landed up safe at the bottom like a little puffball. Her face now was just visible in the gloom . . .

I start to kiss the face, and I start laughing too, as we embrace one another.

We will get ourselves home somehow and I will not think about what is to come. Short views. Today will soon be over: and then there will be tomorrow, and the next day, and perhaps the day after that . . .

15

Quite suddenly, but some time after that eventful journey, I had a breakdown. Shouting and sobbing and screaming. No reason for it.

Iris at first smiled at me incuriously. She did not seem at all surprised. And not very interested either.

What has happened to me? Why have I suddenly popped off? Iris may not be concerned, but I am. I stare dully at myself and say why, why, why.

Abruptly as it seems I realise. Heart has quietly taken itself off. And courage, and will. I can go on doing all the things I have to do, but none of them seem to help us any more.

As the Germans say, *Mut verloren, alles verloren*. I remember Hannelore saying that. She said it in a slightly smug way, when she thought I ought to be bucked up. Typical of a former member of the *Bund deutscher Mädchen*. It annoyed me at the time, but how true it turns out to be.

Guts gone, all gone. That might be the best translation. And I start thinking about that *Mut*. By thinking about it perhaps I can cheer myself up. I remember the Old English poem we all had to study (do they still? – I'm out of touch now) for the English degree.

The Battle of Maldon. In those days too poets preferred heroic failure to brilliant success. The English commander rashly allowed the Vikings to cross the estuary at Maldon, so that the two armies could fight on equal terms. He was killed. Discouragement set in, but a veteran retainer rallies the ranks with a rousing warcry.

Mod sceal the mara the ure megen lytlath. 'Mood shall be the more as our strength wanes'. Am I remembering it right? We can't say 'mood' in the sense of *Mut* any more. Courage, a French word, must have taken us over with the Normans. (The Germans have it too – Mother Courage.)

But what am I doing, trying to cheer myself up with this stuff? No more *Mod*, or *Mut*, in me. I can feel it's all gone. And the English lost the battle.

That ancient defeat seems the last straw. Suddenly I start crying in earnest, gulping and hiccuping, with my mouth gaping open.

At once Iris takes my hand, pats and strokes it. She hardly seems to feel the hand or to know who I am. And yet out of her own absence is she trying to give me comfort? As she could once do, as if she could do it still?

Iris won't eat, is barely drinking. This is a really alarming development. It drives all frivolous thoughts of *Mod* and *Mut* out of my head. For two days she doesn't seem to have had a pee either. (Later, at the home, the nurse tells me that this phase begins when another circuit shuts down in the brain, stopping even the elementary signals that make us urinate, salivate, feel hungry or thirsty.)

Again and again I try a method which has always worked before. She has always let me put little pieces or spoonfuls in her mouth. A dribble of Complan; tiny morsels of toast and honey.

She does not push them away, but her mouth remains closed, like shops on a Sunday morning. As I fed her, only a fortnight ago, I used to say,

'The King was in the counting-house, counting out
    his money,
The Queen was in the parlour, eating bread and
    honey.'

She would respond to my face then, and smile, and the smile made her mouth open easily.

As I go on trying she moves her head sharply, rolling her eyes like a dangerous horse. Before I can stop myself I start to cry again. This time Iris takes no notice.

Rush out of the house and walk round the block by myself. We used to make it last twenty minutes, now it takes hardly any time. I remembered to lock the door on the outside, although I can feel it is hardly necessary now.

A lost frightened feeling about that. As soon as I got used to them I clung desperately to each stage of the disease. The sleeping and forgetting one, the wandering one, the sleepless and distracted one as well. Each soon became a sort of friend.

But now this last one – feeding Iris with a spoon, kissing her when she consents to take a drink – seems to have abandoned us.

When I get back to the house Iris is still huddled at the kitchen table. Mechanically now and without hope I pick up a morsel of honey and bread and put it in a spoon. Without looking she opens her mouth and takes it in. And then smiles at me and makes her old cooing sound.

Dr Jacoby. A kind man, a scholar and a healer: also the knight-errant who has come to our rescue. He visits every few days.

As I talk to him Iris wanders in and out of the room, murmuring something, dragging an old jersey and a dress behind her. The first time he came she had her smile for him and was almost social.

All that is over now. He says the time has come, no doubt about it.

If we can only get to the right place. Vale House is the best. No doubt about that either. It is strictly for cases of need: there is very seldom a vacancy.

'It's harder to get into than Eton,' says Dr Jacoby.

He pauses as if for reflection, and adds – 'or even Winchester.'

His face splits into a grin and we both laugh.

But I at once feel a terrible anxiety. Will I be able to get my little Iris into this great good place? Will she still miss me, will she hate it, want to escape?

As things are now, surely not? And it would be all kindness and care there. The real sort of care which I cannot give.

Dr Jacoby is back next day to say he thinks we'll manage it. A bit of luck – someone has died.

Sheer relief floods through me and I feel myself give a gasp. His dark eyes twinkle at me in such a kindly humorous way. He tells me more about the home. Too dazed to take it in properly, but he is saying it's such a friendly place. No visiting hours. I can spend all day there if I want. All night too.

At last the taxi comes. We have tried ringing for an ambulance and we tried the Medical Centre. Busy at the moment. So sorry. Try again later. 'Far called, our Navies melt away'. The line from Kipling's 'Recessional', presaging the end of Empire, rattles distractedly through my head. Like *Mod* and *Mut*, whose defection has stopped bothering me for the moment. Farstretched our Health Service does its best.

The taxi man looks unperturbed when we tell him the lady is on the stairs and we can't get her down. He comes in with a pleased benevolent look. Glad to help. Kind Frances had come to help too, but even between us we could not get Iris on her feet. Now the taxi man gives her his arm, calls her my love, and she is soon outside and looking happy. I ask the taxi man about his taxi's doors. Yes, they are locked. Frances waves, and gets into her car.

Suddenly a marvellous peace and quiet. I hold Iris's hand and we smile shyly and happily at each other. The last ride together. Like Anna Karenina's to the railway station.

But it feels more as if we had just got married, or as if we were just going to get married and were going in the taxi together to the Registrar, holding hands.

*   *   *

[277]

Trouble getting out. But a nurse takes a gentle hold of Iris's no longer reluctant fingers. The finger-tips of both hands. Walking slowly backwards, Maureen – her name is on her overall – leads Iris to a door. A smile on her face now, and on Iris's too. They process slowly and with a happy concentration, as if treading an informal minuet together.

Through the door and into Vale House. I have lost track of *Mod* and *Mut* and our Navies melting away, and find myself clinging now to another sort of joke, one I cannot share with Iris, with whom I would have shared it once, or with the staff, who are so kind and helpful. It is the memory of Mrs Gamp in Dickens, and her 'Wale', the Vale of Tears in which we are all destined to live. In any age.

But this nice casual house does not look like a 'Wale'. Warmth, brightness, more kind faces, and the lounge where patients are sitting as if in a snug old-fashioned hotel. They pay us no attention, but one or two seem to see us with benign passive incuriosity.

Iris's smile transforms her own face now. She is among fellows and friends, still more of Dr A's friends. She does not look back as she enters the room, and I can see that she is still smiling.

Iris died in Vale House on February the eighth 1999. The reassurance I and all those other friends could not give her had come at last. This was the best of the friends.

She had grown steadily weaker. Without bother or fuss, as if someone she trusted had helped her to come to a decision, she stopped eating and drinking. Gentle pressure from those kind nurses but no insistence. No horror of being put on a drip.

During the last week she took to opening her blue eyes very wide, as if merrily. Her face was still round and beautiful, although the body I held in my arms was shrunken and light. When she died I closed her eyes and then opened them, as if we could still play together. She had looked and not seen us for days, but now she seemed to see me.

Tricia O'Leary, the head of the home, came in. She was crying, rather to my surprise, as she must have seen this happen a great many times before. But they had all come to love Iris very much.

Dying had been so quiet that I found myself saying to Tricia, 'I wouldn't mind doing that myself.' She smiled and took my hand and Maureen brought me a cup of strong tea.

I thought thankfully of those 'few words' no one was going to have to say at a funeral or a Memorial Service. Iris had told me years back that she didn't want either. She had been firm about that. So there would be a Wake instead, a big party for all her friends.

I don't care for that word 'carer', just because it has become so unavoidable.

And the gap caring leaves when it stops is unavoidable too. A month ago I wrote in my diary: how will I get through the time when I am not looking after Iris?

And as if to cheat emptiness, when it should come, I took care to anticipate. The moments I then looked forward to all day – my drink, my book over supper – would cease to mean anything. They would vanish like a puff of smoke.

And have they vanished? I am still finding out. Remember the Law of the Conservation of Pleasure? Has it become a law of consolation? Not so much a law as a fact.

In this numbed and vacant time our old friend Belial is the first to call with his condolences. He is no more to be avoided than the undertaker. Those thoughts that wander through eternity. And Belial himself, who speaks up for them in *Paradise Lost* with such eloquence, he is still around. A comic figure but a persistent one. I can't shut him up and tell him to go away.

Iris never knew him personally. He only came into our lives after she became ill. But what he brought to us both we can still share.

Because he resembles another, even older friend. The friend who arrived unexpectedly when we fell in love. It was at that dance in the summer of 1954, when we babbled to each other for hours, upstairs in my little room at St Antony's. Thanks to that friend we had a new language to speak, a language which we spoke together as if by instinct.

I have since thought about what then seemed to come so naturally. I have thought: here I am married to the most intelligent woman in England, and we have never had a serious conversation. We never talk to each other in a way that would be intelligible to anyone else. Or worth listening to if it was.

We are still talking in that way, and I shall never leave

home now. Home is Iris and Iris is home. Dr Alzheimer was a friend who never stopped Iris talking to me, nor I to her.

I don't miss her. Perhaps because I don't remember her. Not in the way that I remember things and people in the past. No wonder Iris wanted no Memorial Service. She knew I would not need to remember her. She was not present at the party given in her honour. She stayed at home, and I could not wait to get back to her.

When we left home in former times, before Iris became ill, she was always there to look after me. She enjoyed that. She enjoyed getting the tickets at the station, paying the taxi, steering me through the caverns of the Underground. She kept me safe. And she will still do that at home, the place where in those days I used to look after her.

Bereavement means a tearing away. But we and Belial know it as a comic word. I play with it now, as I used to play with the word 'Alzheimer'. In my mind's eye – Belial's eye – I can see this bereaved person. A grave party, in a smooth furry top-hat. A beaver hat.

I shall linger with him under the benign sky, and wonder how anyone could imagine unquiet slumbers for the sleeper in that quiet bed. The bed where Iris is lying with her martial cloak around her. As she used to do in the evenings when I tucked her up as she was, because I could not persuade her to let me take her clothes off. And so I recited 'The Burial of Sir John Moore' to her instead. And then she always smiled up at me.

I sleep quietly now, with Iris quiet beside me. I drop

off in the daytime too, and wake up feeling calm and cheerful as if Iris had been there.

But jokes can show us the truth – too much so – as well as bringing back the past. That last joke, the one Anna Karenina never told.

This morning I caught the tail of my vest again on the windsor chair, coming up with my mug of tea. I wanted to tell Iris about it, and the funny things that had happened in my memory after I had first caught my tail, that morning a year ago. But when I got upstairs I found she was not there, and I could not tell her.